Joy

The Journey Home

Deacon Bill Rich

iUniverse, Inc.
Bloomington

Joy
The Journey Home

Scripture quotations contained herein are from the New Revised Standard Version (NRSV) Bible, copyright © 1989 by the Division of Christian Education of the National Council of the Churches of Christ in the U.S.A., and are used by permission. All rights reserved.

iUniverse books may be ordered through booksellers or by contacting:

iUniverse
1663 Liberty Drive
Bloomington, IN 47403
www.iuniverse.com
1-800-Authors (1-800-288-4677)

Because of the dynamic nature of the Internet, any web addresses or links contained in this book may have changed since publication and may no longer be valid. The views expressed in this work are solely those of the author and do not necessarily reflect the views of the publisher, and the publisher hereby disclaims any responsibility for them.

Any people depicted in stock imagery provided by Thinkstock are models, and such images are being used for illustrative purposes only.

Certain stock imagery © Thinkstock.

ISBN: 978-1-4697-5800-8 (sc)
ISBN: 978-1-4697-5801-5 (e)

Printed in the United States of America

iUniverse rev. date: 4/30/2012

Table of Contents

Preface

I have written this book for many reasons. I wanted to share the gift I have experienced on the chance it might help others find their way home. I also wanted a simple explanation of Roman Catholicism for those interested in making a journey similar to mine. However, the most important reason I wrote this book is it was the only way I could stop being hounded by the idea of doing so.

There have been many contributors to this effort.

I believe the inspiration came from God, and it is with his grace I have written. As one example, notice the number of times a particular piece of information appeared just when I needed it. I don't think this says anything about me, other than that I was willing.

I struggled with the question of citing Scripture references or including entire passages at the beginning of many chapters. In the end I remembered my own experience. Having avoided the Bible most of my life, it was only with great reluctance that I finally opened one while working on our first teen retreat. I soon discovered that a little practice rapidly changed my willingness to start exploring the Bible more fully. I hope readers will make the effort to look up and read the referenced passages so they may experience the same awakening. Seek and you will find.

All Scripture references in this book come from the New Revised Standard Version (NRSV), Catholic Edition. The choice is primarily personal. My favorite biblical scholar, Donald Senior, president of the Catholic Theological Union, uses the NSRV, Catholic Edition. When scripture sources are referenced in footnotes, I have used the following abbreviations for Gospel authors: MT = Matthew, MK = Mark, LK = Luke and JN = John.

All references to the Catechism come from the *Catechism of the Catholic Church, Second Edition, revised in accordance with the official Latin text promulgated by Pope John Paul II*. I am also indebted to Richard Rohr, author of several books and audiotapes that have had a strong influence on my thinking, and John Powell, S.J., author of a daily meditation book called *Through Seasons of the Heart*. This book was given to me at my ordination in 1987, and I think I have read a passage from it almost every day since. More often than I care to admit, I have discovered what I had thought was an original idea of mine in one of his daily reflections. Finally, my first book, *Scattered Raindrops,* not only gave me the confidence to attempt a second book but influenced much of my thinking in its writing.

I love to make notes as I read something interesting. As an aid to those who may have the same inclination, I have made a conscious effort to leave sufficient blank space throughout the book. I hope you find it helpful.

There is no way to adequately express how grateful I am for all those who helped form me once I began my spiritual journey in earnest. In so many ways my story is their story, my beliefs the lessons they have taught me. From Jim Ray, who first described the Jesuit "Why Not?" formula, to all those who challenged me with their questions, heartfelt sharing, trust, and even their complaints. I have been formed by these interactions in so many ways. This book would not have been possible without them.

In particular, I am indebted to Fr. Art Venezia for his invaluable suggestions after reading the manuscript. I am also grateful for the support and friendship of all the priests I have had the privilege of knowing, including Fr. Charlie, Fr. Dave B., Fr. David R., Fr. Tom, Fr. Gavin, Fr. Tim O., Fr. Tim L., Fr. Michael, Fr. Edmund, Fr. David C., Fr. Tony, Msgr. Jim and Fr. Art.

Finally, I thank Frannie. For fifty years of marriage. For teaching me the importance of honest communications. For putting up with and supporting the writing of this book in so many ways. In my opinion, she is living proof of the goodness of God.

Dedication

For all those willing to seek,
because they will find.

I say these things to you
So my joy may be in you
And your joy may be complete.
JN 15:11

I
Why Bother?

On Being Catholic

I love being Catholic. Roman Catholic. It has helped me figure out who and why I am, what's important and not important. It has helped me live life more completely, with a greater sense of joy.

Now, don't get me wrong. I am not what most would consider a model Catholic. I don't attend Mass every day. I rarely pray the Rosary. I don't follow all the rules. I don't even know all the rules. Until I decided to write this book, I had never bothered to look at a Catechism. Besides, I have never done very well with authority. I was once voted the person least likely to do what he was told to do.

I was baptized a Catholic at a very early age. But for a good part of my life, I thought of Roman Catholicism as out of touch with reality and hopelessly mired in the past. The journey to where I am today began because a priest invited parishioners over the age of twenty-five to play basketball one night a week. I decided to go because I figured we would probably go out and drink beer afterwards.

And yet, here I am. Who says miracles don't happen anymore?

Many Dwelling Places

It tickles me whenever someone says to me something like "You Catholics always...." One of the great fictions concerning Roman Catholicism is that there is ONE kind of Catholic. We all do exactly as we are told, believe exactly the same things, have exactly the same perception of Jesus, pray the same way, and want the same things. Nothing could be further from the truth. Jesus told his apostles that his Father's house had many dwelling places.[1] Metaphorically, the space for Catholics has many dwellings. We have conservative Catholics who still pine for the Latin Mass, liberal Catholics who wonder why we ever pray or sing anything in Latin; feminists who believe women need a more formal role in the Church hierarchy; equally devoted women who are convinced of the opposite; charismatics who love a lively worship service, others who prefer just the reverse. If there were a poll among American Catholics on a variety of Catholic teachings, I strongly suspect there would be a whole range of responses. I could go on and on without ever mentioning the fact that as a global religion, the common faith of Catholicism is internalized by every culture in its own unique way. As John Powell states in *Seasons of the Heart*, we are all fractions, in the process of becoming whole numbers.[2] We all tend to find the Divine in slightly different ways.

This lesson came home to me in a personal way when I started meeting people whom I felt had a well-developed spirituality. You may have met one or more of them. They are the men and woman who exude a calm joy in their approach to life. Whenever I have the opportunity to talk with someone like this (I always want what they have), I am struck by the different images of of the Divine they have as well as the variety of experiences that led to them to where they are. A Parish administrator helped me understand this phenomenon when she had everyone on our Parish staff take the Myers-Briggs personality test. She wanted to show that even members of a Parish staff, convinced we were all the same, have different ways of approaching and assimilating reality.

All of which shouldn't surprise anyone. Think of your own family. Aren't there distinctive differences among the various members?

So, if you have an image of what a Catholic is and are concerned you might not fit in, don't worry. What you are seeing is one of many

---

1   JN 14:2
2   Seasons of the Heart, p. 106

Catholics. Search, and you will find. Besides, the vast majority is just like you, trying to find a better way to live each day.

What I Love

I love the Mass. I love the feeling of continuity, community, and connectedness to the Divine. The whole idea of the Real Presence is breathtaking to me. Add good music, and I am reduced to tears. I feel at home.

I live in awe of priests who live their vocation. The ones who do the best they can to live as Christ would have them live. The ones who are faithful to their vows: willing to make the ongoing sacrifices required of any priest trying to be present to his parishioners and yet do so with a sense of humility and humor.

I am at home with the basic principles of Roman Catholicism, the core beliefs. They give my life meaning and a purpose. They help me know what is real. And what is not.

I love the continuity of the church. The sense of mystery in its various ceremonies. The sameness, adjusted for local cultural influences, wherever I go. The framework for living provided by an ongoing hierarchy. And a Tradition that links me all the way back to the apostles.

Most of all, I think, I love the notion of the Body of Christ: you and me and all those willing to make the effort to recognize the presence of the Divine in our midst. To struggle together, imperfectly, sometimes in laughter, sometimes in frustration, sometimes in tears, but together. To care for—and sometimes to curse—each other, to be family. To give meaning to the promise "I am with you always, to the end of the age."[3]

All of this has come to have such great meaning for me for a simple reason. Roman Catholicism has taught me how to experience true joy.

---

3 MT 28:20

Joy

I think I started using this word over twenty years ago. I am not sure, because I didn't even realize it until much later, when a parishioner stopped me cold by asking what I meant. Surprisingly, I found I couldn't answer the question. How does one describe being fully alive? Or colors to someone who has never seen them? I was speechless—a very rare condition for me—and I started to keep a journal to discover just what I meant.

First, I know that I am loved, and that I am lovable. It is good to be me: just the way I am. In all the counseling I have been privileged to do, I have found that this, accepting one's self-worth, is THE NARROW GATE through which one must pass to live life more fully. It certainly was a difficult passage for me, with a number of stumbling blocks along the way.

I know I am never alone. That a power far greater than I knows me better than I know myself, knows what is best for me, better than I know what's best for me, and is always with me, in me, helping me become all I can be. This power is present in every breath I breathe, every thought I think, every action I take. Answered prayers are a reality. I am never alone.

I am grateful for what I have, right now, today. For everything I can see, feel, hear, touch, and taste. Above all, I am grateful for my relationships, particularly my wife, my family and close friends, the people who have taken the time to care. They lift my soul and make me more. I can't tell you how often I say to myself, "How did I get so lucky?" My most common prayer is a simple "Thank you, Jesus."

I feel joy whenever I take time to share with others. I always feel I get more than I give. When asked why I like being a permanent deacon, my answer is simple: "I love being a deacon because I'm selfish. I like to feel good. "

Of course, life still happens. There are problems, irritations, disappointments, even tragedies when loved ones pass away, have debilitating diseases, or, for whatever reason, simply walk away. I still make mistakes, many and repeated. It is almost impossible for me to remember where I leave things, lose enough weight, keep track of people's names, or stay focused on the subject of the moment when an interesting thought strikes me. When I expect others to behave as I think they should, I am almost always disappointed. I have cancer, a chronic back problem, and a debilitating form of psoriasis on the palms of my hands and the soles of my feet. Life happens.

The difference is that I now have a much better idea how to deal with life. I don't have to be perfect; I just have to be me. It is better to accept others as they are rather than as I would have them. Emotions, both good and bad, will pass and can be replaced by my attitudes, one of the very few things I control completely.

There is almost always some good news in every situation. Laughter works wonders. So do the occasional tears. I am only responsible for the effort. Results take care of themselves. Worry, anxiety, and remorse are nothing more than wasted time and energy. When I let him, God will always bring good from whatever trouble, disappointment, or crisis I encounter. For, you see, I know the end of the story. I believe in resurrections.

I am content. I am free. I feel good in my own skin.

That's what I mean when I say "joy." In John's Gospel, Jesus called it eternal life. Life that begins as soon as we come to know the only true God and the one he sent.[4] Knowing someone or something is not a casual endeavor. It takes time and it takes effort. But, as with other promises Jesus made, what I have experienced has taught me eternal life is my choice, my reality, and my future.

Of course, as is my wont, once I had this list, I began to wonder. Is this real? Or am I kidding myself? After all, what is happiness? I was listening to NPR as I pondered these questions one day. By coincidence, the person being interviewed was a research psychologist, Sonja Lyubomirsky, who had just written a book called *The How of Happiness: A Scientific Approach to Getting the Life You Want*. A book on happiness. Just what I needed! I went out and bought the book that day.

I guess I shouldn't have been surprised by the list of Ms. Lybomirsky's "hows." Her research was impressive, and I mean to take nothing away from her, but it sounded to me like she'd read the Gospels. Here I would like to focus on three of her conclusions.

First, based on years of work, the author concluded that these were "the thinking and behavior patterns of the happiest participants in our studies:

- They devote a great deal of time to their family and friends, nurturing and enjoying those relationships.
- They are comfortable expressing gratitude for all they have.

---

4   John 17:3

- They are often the first to offer helping hands to coworkers and passersby.
- They practice optimism when imagining their futures.
- They savor life's pleasures and try to live in the present moment.
- They make physical exercise a weekly and even daily habit.
- They are deeply committed to lifelong goals and ambitions (e.g. fighting fraud, building cabinets, or teaching their children their deeply held   values).
- Last but not least, the happiest people do have their share of stresses, crises, and even tragedies. They may become just as distressed and emotional in such circumstances as you or I, but their secret weapon is the poise and strength they show in coping in the face of the challenge."[5]

I wrote my description of "Joy" before reading that book. Once I did, I realized I had forgotten to emphasize sufficiently the importance of my wife in my life.

But what about all the stuff we typically associate with the drive to happiness: material wealth, privileged position, and being attractive? "Perhaps the most counterintuitive finding is…only about 10% of the variance in happiness levels is explained by differences in life circumstances or situations—that is, whether we are rich or poor, healthy or unhealthy, beautiful or plain, etc."[6] My first reaction when I read this was wishing someone had told me a long time ago so I hadn't had to waste so much energy figuring it out for myself. And then, it dawned on me; someone had, back in my early religion classes. It just took me way too long, and a surprising number of false starts, to accept this simple truth.

Just in case you are wondering whether happiness or joy or whatever you choose to call it is something worth pursuing, I leave you with this thought. In her foreword, Ms Lyubomirsky states, "Working on how to become happier, the research suggests, will not only make a person *feel* better, but will also boost his or her energy, creativity, and immune system, foster better relationships, fuel higher productivity at work, and even lead to a longer life. Happiness, in my humble opinion, is the Holy Grail, 'the meaning and purpose of life,' as Aristotle famously said, 'the whole aim and

---

5   *The How of Happiness,* Sonja Lyubomirsky, p.22
6   Ibid, p. 21

end of existence."[7] If you saw that quotation as a TV ad for a product guaranteed to produce the desired result, what would you be willing to pay for it?

These are the kinds of things the Jesus of my understanding focused on, talked about, and made possible. This is what my Roman Catholicism has helped me find.

---

7   Ibid, p. 2

So, Why Bother?

There are many ways to look at the size of various religious denominations in the United States. While there has been a significant trend away from church attendance in all major Christian denominations, most would agree that the individual denomination with the greatest losses in people over eighteen years old is Roman Catholicism. "Catholicism has experienced the greatest net losses as a result of affiliation changes. While nearly one-in-three Americans (31%) were raised in the Catholic faith, today fewer than one-in-four (24%) describe themselves as Catholic."[8] Said another way, when you count participants by specific denomination rather than aggregating them as "evangelical" or "black churches" or "Protestant," the largest single denomination in this country is "non-practicing Catholics." Fifty-six percent, or 35.9 million, of all American Roman Catholics attend Mass a few times a year or never.[9] The second largest denomination, of course, is made up of "practicing Catholics", approximately 24 to thirty million, depending upon whose survey is used. The third largest, Southern Baptist, has approximately 16.5 million members, or something less than that if only those who regularly attend church services are counted. [10]

Non-practicing Catholics do not tend to migrate to other traditional Protestant faith traditions. They move nowhere (the majority) or to some form of congregation with minimal formal rules. They have plenty of choices: statistics from J. Gordon Melton's *Encyclopedia of American Religion* indicate that the number of denominations had risen to 2650 as of 2003. Other reports[11] indicate there are over 6200 religious denominations in the United States. And this number appears to be currently increasing almost geometrically.[12] It seems many people are searching for the right fit and having a hard time finding it, searching for what they feel is the perfect form of organized religion, when in reality no such thing exists. In fact, I would contend the primary determinant of what faith tradition holds the greatest potential for offering spiritual growth is the one you were exposed to as a young child.

---

8   The Pew Forum, US Religious Landscape Survey
9   Center for Applied Research in the Apostolate, Georgetown University
10   Adherents.com: National and World Religions Statistics
11   World Christian Encyclopedia
12   USA Today, Jan. 23, 2003

For reasons I cannot fully explain, I have spent a great deal of time over the past twenty years with "former" or what I call "unchurched churched" (attending Mass with no interest or understanding) Catholics. Very few have a satisfying spiritual life. Most avoid the subject, perhaps because they feel spiritual growth is unimportant or unattainable. The ones who are willing to talk about it are quick to point out that there is a big difference between religion (undefined but misguided) and spirituality (countless definitions). What strikes me most about these people, however, is their deep but unsatisfied hunger to live life more fully, without knowing the only path to enduring happiness is a spiritual path.

The reasons Roman Catholics leave the church are interesting. For a very small number there are particularly painful and understandable reasons. Serious mistakes made by a priest or a nun causing significant harm. The resulting rejection of the Church is unfortunate but understandable. Surprisingly, the people I have met in this category show a remarkable willingness to set aside the past in an effort to discover whether Catholicism can still have meaning for them.

For the vast majority of those leaving, however, their reasons seem to be grounded in the feeling that nothing positive has been gained from their religious experience, combined with an aversion to finding out why. This conviction is expressed in many different ways: disagreement with a particular teaching of the church, encounters with an insensitive priest, an almost instinctive rejection of a fear-based and obligation-based image of God acquired in childhood, the belief the Mass is boring and/or out of date, or just the all-too-human tendency to think "I can do better on my own."

The question "So, why bother?" has two sides. The first side: Why have I bothered to try and write this book? Answer: I believe to the core of my being that the best path to joy is a spiritual path and that for nonpracticing or sometime Catholics the best way to travel that path is almost certainly Roman Catholicism. I believe this because it has been my experience. For almost fifteen years I rejected Catholicism, for most of the reasons cited in the last paragraph. Since my spiritual journey began in earnest, I have spent countless hours with other non-practicing or semi-practicing Catholics. The results have always been the same. Anyone who makes the effort to practice rather than observe his or her faith tradition grows and becomes more. Practice takes effort. Practice takes understanding.

But it always yields results. It's one of God's promises.[13] I hope this book will help those who would like to give it a try. Besides, I know that whatever else happens, I will learn more in the writing of this book than will any reader in the reading. Another promise: about receiving more than you give.[14]

The other side of the question, "So, why bother?" is for you, the reader. Why should you bother reading this book? In asking this question I am bold enough to include most practicing Catholics, because most currently practicing Catholics do so with only a minimal understanding of their faith tradition. Most churchgoing Catholics ended their religious education somewhere between second and seventh grade. How would you like to go through life with a second-grade education?

The answer to the question "So, why bother?" seems simple enough to me. What have you got to lose? A little time. And just maybe the draining search for meaning and contentment in your life. What have you to gain? Potentially, everything.

Consider that an invitation in the spirit of the disciples' initial encounter with Jesus as told in the Gospel of John. When Jesus turned and saw them following, he said, "What are you looking for?" They said to him, "'Rabbi' (which means teacher), 'where are you staying?' He said to them, 'Come, and you will see.'"[15]

What are you looking for?

Come, and you will see.

---

13   LK 11:9
14   LK 6:38
15   JN 1:38-39

II
Lights Along the Path

In Brief

God is.
God is love.
God calls us to love.
God leads us to love.

These statements summarize the fundamental beliefs of Roman Catholicism. These are what one must accept if he or she wants to become a member of our faith tradition. Everything else that makes up Roman Catholicism flows from them. Everything else takes on clarity and beauty once these ideas are integrated into one's life. I would like to say "simple" ideas, but then there is nothing simple about love.

The Catechism calls these truths and the resulting teachings "lights along the path of faith."[16]

It also states "the whole concern of doctrine and its teaching must be directed to the love that never ends....The love of our Lord must always be made accessible, so that anyone can see that all the works of perfect Christian virtue spring from love and have no other objective than to arrive at love."[17]

16   Catechism, 89
17   Catechism, 25

God Is

God is

Not was or will be, but is. Not there but here. Not sometimes but always. God is.

When Moses asked God for his name, the reply was "I AM WHO I AM."[18] I AM means the present. Unfortunately, we spend too much of our time regretting the past or worrying about the future. Nothing you regret or worry about can alter either the past or the future. Can any of you add a single moment to your life by worrying?[19]

If you want to know this God who is, start by spending more time in the present.

God can be found only in the present, for only the present is eternal.

God is the only God

There are no other gods. No other god loves. No other god satisfies. God is the only God because...

God is real

The most profound realization of the earliest Jewish believers was a simple one: God is real. He actually exists. Unlike other gods, he was part of the people's lived experience. He interacted with them, made promises to them, led them out of slavery, left them to their own devices when they were unfaithful, forgave them, and was with them always. He loved them. There had never before been a god like this.

Many centuries later, the earliest followers of Jesus were struck by this same reality: God is real. He had raised Jesus from the dead, and this risen Jesus had become part of the lived experience of ongoing Christian communities. Through his victory over death, Jesus represented "an encounter with a hope..., a hope which transformed life and the world from within."[20]

Many centuries later, the only way we can truly come to believe that God is real—in the gut, and the heart, as well as in the head—is to find him in our own lived experience. To discover he is cause for hope because resurrections are real; that we too can be led from whatever enslaves us to freedom.

---

18 Exodus 3:14
19 MT 6:27
20 Spe Salvi, p.5

The most common way many of us first experience the Divine is through the loving care of parents with an active faith. Of course, there are countless other ways we can experience God: an inexplicable coincidence that produces a momentary feeling of joy, a sense of peace while praying, the unexplainable well-being that surfaces when we forego our own pleasure to help another, that moment when we turn to God and surrender completely because nothing else has worked. The common denominator in all these experiences is they all occur in the present. Experiences such as these are the only way we know for sure God actually exists, that he is real.

God is almighty

God is without limits. Without beginning and without end. He alone is perfect: knowledge, wisdom, truth, and life complete, beyond the bounds of time and space. He is whole, holy.

He transcends our capacity to comprehend or adequately describe. As such, he is more than known revelation, more than any one religion. Neither male nor female, he is more than either or both. There are no words to adequately describe the Divine. He is beyond the limitations of language and our imagination.

I believe the greatest disservice we who claim to be believers do is to impose our limitations on God. When we do, we diminish the grandeur of God and ourselves. Richard Dawkins, a well-known evolutionary biologist, atheist, and author of *The Ancestor's Tale* and *The God Delusion,* said it very well: "My objection to supernatural beliefs is precisely that they fail to do justice to the sublime grandeur of the real world. I suspect many who call themselves religious would find themselves agreeing with me. To them I would quote a favorite remark from...a distinguished elder statesman... 'You know, we really do agree. It's just you say it wrong.'"[21] While I disagree with Mr. Dawkins' underlying premise, I think we give well-intentioned intelligent people like him far too much fodder when we try to limit the Divine with our preconceived notions.

While God is infinitely greater than all his creation, he is also intimately present in and to us. I think this is the greatest of the mysteries we encounter when dealing with the Divine. He can be totally other, the creator of a universe so vast it is difficult to get our minds around, and, at the same time, be individually and uniquely present in each of us. "In him we live and move and have our being....

---

21   Richard Dawkins, The Ancestor's Tale, p.614

At every moment he upholds and sustains us...."[22] Through him, we and all his creation exist, *God in all things.* With him, we and all creation have the potential to become more. *All things in God.*[23]

He is both intimately present and totally other. Nothing is impossible with God.[24] God is almighty.[25]

22   Catechism, 300
23   God in all things, all things in God: I can't remember where I first heard this but I think it originated with St. Ignatius.
24   LK 1:37
25   Catechism, 272

God Is Love

God is love

"Love is from God; everyone who loves is born of God and knows God. Whoever does not love does not know God, for God is love."[26] "By love, God has revealed himself and given himself to man."[27] "God is love, and love is his first gift, containing all others."[28] As such, God's caring, compassion, and forgiveness are complete and without condition. Beyond our ability to fully comprehend. Beyond our ability to even imagine.

STOP! Reread that last paragraph. Reread it again. This simple statement is so hard to integrate into our consciousness because we experience it so rarely. But if you take only one thing from this book, take this: God is love.

Love creates

God is the source of all. He created everything that exists, seen and unseen, in love. In this statement lie the answers to our most basic questions: "Where do we come from? Where are we going? What is our origin? What is our end?"[29]

God's creation is good. "He saw everything he had made, and indeed, it was very good."[30] We were created in goodness and are inherently good. Of all the worlds he could have created, he created this one, with you just as you are, and me just as I am. He created each one of us as a completely unique expression of his love. There is no other you or me. And he loves us without condition just as we are. Struggling to become more, but as we are.

As Arlo Guthrie used to say, "Hard to believe!" But if you doubt your uniqueness, try and find one other person with your fingerprints, your exact voice, your DNA, your exact kind of intelligence. If you doubt whether you are inherently good, whether you are a gift, just keep reading.

By the way, God's creative power is still at work. Creation is ongoing.

---

26   1 John 4:7-8
27   Catechism, 68
28   Catechism, 733
29   Catechism, 282
30   Genesis 1:31

Love requires choice

"God created humankind in his image, in the image of God he created them; male and female he created them."[31] Of all God's creation, only we are able to know and love God.[32] This is true because we are spiritual beings. [33] We are spiritual beings learning how to be human. We have been given the gift of free will, the ability to think, to ponder the past and future, and make choices. Without choice, there is no love.

We are not yet complete. God has placed within each of us a desire for completeness. An emptiness that can only be filled by what we call joy or infinite happiness. God has placed this yearning in our hearts to draw us to him. "Only in God will we find the truth and happiness we never stop searching for..." because only in God can we become complete, whole, holy. God alone satisfies.[34]

God's will for us is that we learn to live in complete joy, because God is love. Only love can complete us. Love alone satisfies.

Created in God's image, we will live forever. Eternal life is life lived fully on the path to life lived completely in union with the Divine. Forever. It is our choice.

There can be no choice, no free will, without the potential for evil. The story of Adam and Eve reveals that the origin of evil involves bad choices, a misuse of free will. God did not create evil; we did.

Because we are imperfect, we make mistakes. God is perfect. We are not. God is all-knowing. We are not. God is judge. We are not. God is the creator. We are not. Too often we overlook these realities.

Love reveals

Love makes itself known to those loved. God reveals himself to us so we can come to know the fullness of his love.

God has revealed and continues to reveal his love in three ways: Holy Scripture, Tradition, and individual inspiration. Sacred Scripture and Tradition are the twin pillars of God's revelation of his love to the entire Church. Together they are called the "Sacred Deposit of the Faith." Individual inspiration is, as its name implies, personal in nature.

---

31 Genesis 1:27
32 Catechism, 356
33 Catechism, 365
34 Catechism, 27, 1718

Scripture includes the entire Bible as understood by Roman Catholics, including the unity of the Old and New Testaments. The Gospels are the heart of all the Scriptures. God is the author of Sacred Scripture through inspiration provided to its authors. Sacred Scripture teaches the truth. Christ, through the Holy Spirit, opens our minds to understand Scripture in terms relevant to us today.[35]

Sacred Scripture constitutes the totality of public revelation, meaning that it fully discloses God's plan for humankind's salvation through his son, Jesus Christ. There will be no further public revelation until Jesus returns in glory.

Interpretation of Holy Scripture is ongoing, just as creation is ongoing.

Tradition means that the Holy Spirit continues to provide inspiration and guidance (let us call this continuing revelation) to aid us in fully comprehending the mystery of God's love revealed in Holy Scripture. By its very nature, Tradition can never contradict Holy Scripture. The bishops and the Pope, as successors to the original apostles, are responsible for discerning the content of this guidance in matters affecting the entire church. The results of this discernment constitute the living and growing Tradition of Roman Catholicism.

Tradition (as well as our organizational structure) has its source in the principle of Apostolic Succession, meaning that Jesus selected twelve apostles, imparting to them special graces needed for the celebration of Sacraments, discernment of God's ongoing revelation, and teaching of the faithful. These graces are then transmitted to succeeding generations of apostles (bishops) and, in a limited way, to their ordained assistants (priests and, to a lesser extent, deacons) over time. As an aside, Apostolic Succession is also at the heart of almost all differences between Roman Catholicism and other Christian denominations, based on perceived abuses by the Papacy in the Middle Ages.

Many of our most important beliefs are based on Tradition. For example, while the idea of a Trinitarian God is present in Holy Scripture, the word "Trinity" is never mentioned. Similarly, there is no discussion of Sacraments as we currently understand them or the role of Mary in the Church or the Communion of Saints, to name a few examples. These Traditions are called dogmas. Think of a dogma as the expression of divinely revealed truth by the Church based on an evolving understanding of Holy Scripture.

35   Catechism, 105, 125

Traditions should not be confused with the many traditions (habits formed over time by local churches) or teachings of the Church (e.g., artificial contraception). In both cases, notice the small "t."

A summary of the early and most basic Traditions can be found in *The Creed,* which we profess every Sunday. Interestingly, many Protestant churches, which disagree with the idea of Tradition, profess the same Creed.

An example may help understand what a Tradition is and how it comes into being. The primary point in the example is the Pope and a few bishops do not get together and dream up something. In fact, God's revelation comes through the People of God, often referred to as the laity, and happens over a relatively long period of time. The Pope and his bishops must then discern true guidance from God versus various local traditions. In this effort, they are always cautious about interpreting, applying and recognizing Traditions.

The feast of the Immaculate Conception, meaning that Mary was conceived without sin, is a Tradition of the Roman Catholic Church. It is an interesting example because, unlike Traditions such as the Trinity, the nature of Jesus, or the Eucharist, it is a relatively recent Tradition. In addition, it cannot easily be tied to a specific reference from Holy Scripture.

No one is certain how the belief started, although there are several theories. What is known is that during the first centuries of the second millennia, the belief that Mary had been conceived without sin became widespread in Catholic communities, so much so that in 1476, Pope Sixtus IV made it a Feast Day, proclaiming it to be a teaching of the Church. In 1545, The Council of Trent reaffirmed it as a teaching of the Church.

By the mid-1800s the belief was almost universal. As a result, Pope Pius IX, in concert with his fellow bishops, finally decided the Immaculate Conception was official Dogma (meaning it became a Tradition) in 1854, using as his Scriptural source references to Mary as "full of grace" and "highly favored." In 1858, four years later, Mary appeared to a young peasant girl named Bernadette Soubirous in Lourdes, France. Mary introduced herself by saying, "I am the Immaculate Conception."

In addition to Holy Scripture and Tradition, God also reveals himself to every individual who seeks him in good conscience and with an open heart. "When you search for me, you will find me; if you seek me with all your heart, I will let you find me, says the Lord."

[36] "Ask, and it will be given to you; search, and you will find; knock, and the door will be opened for you. For everyone who asks receives, and everyone who searches finds, and for everyone who knocks, the doors will be opened."[37] Personal inspiration depends on the openness of the individual to Divine help and varies based on the needs of the individual. Personal inspiration can never contradict properly interpreted Sacred Scripture and Tradition.

Love is relational

God's creation is interdependent. All creatures are related, meaning no creature is self-sufficient. Humans are not solitary creatures. We come to know ourselves, the world around us, the meaning of life, and the reality of love, in relationship. Relationships are important.

God himself is relational, containing three discrete but related elements: Father, Son or Word, and the Holy Spirit. "The mystery of the Holy Trinity is the central mystery of Christian faith and life. It is therefore the source of all other mysteries of faith, the light that enlightens them. It is the most fundamental and essential teaching in the 'hierarchy of truths.'"[38] The Trinity is one God. The Divine elements, or "persons," of the Trinity are truly distinct from one another, yet one. The Father is related to the Son, the Son to the Father, and the Holy Spirit to both. While it is impossible for us to understand, think of love: Love creates (Father), fosters and reveals (Son or Word), and sustains (Holy Spirit). Love is one mysterious reality, with distinct but related characteristics.

The Father relates to his ongoing creation in two ways.

---

36   Jeremiah 29:13-14
37   MT 7:7-8
38   Catechism, 234

God Calls Us to Love

Jesus is the Word

Jesus was begotten by God and is one with God. He is "consubstantial" with the Father, meaning he is of the same substance or nature as the Father. As the definitive Word of God, Jesus was present at the beginning of creation, when God "spoke" creation into being.[39] Jesus is fully divine.

Jesus is God's Word made man

At the time of God's choosing, Jesus became man through the power of the Holy Spirit in concert with the Virgin Mary. Jesus lived, was tempted, suffered, and died as a man. Jesus was fully human.

Jesus is God's gift of love to the world. In taking on human form, Jesus confirmed humankind's inherent goodness. Jesus was like us in all things but sin.

Jesus calls us to love

During his public ministry, Jesus called us to love God and our neighbor as ourselves. He taught us how to love through his teachings and by various signs. He proclaimed the Good News of his Father's Kingdom, which he initiated through the power of the Holy Spirit. He taught that enduring happiness is found only in conforming our lives to the will of the Father.

Shortly before his death, Jesus washed his apostles' feet, a task normally reserved for the most menial servant. He then gave them his final commandment: "As my Father has loved me, so I have loved you. Abide in my love. If you keep my commandments, you will abide in my love....I have said these things to you so that my joy may be in you, and that your joy may be complete. This is my commandment, that you love one another as I have loved you."[40]

Jesus also called us to love by dying for us. There is no greater love than the willingness to give one's life for another.[41] Jesus freely sacrificed himself as atonement for sin and to usher in a new age based on forgiveness. In doing so, He freed us from the power of sin. He died, was buried, and was raised from the dead so that we might have eternal life. The power of love will always triumph.

---

39 Genesis 1
40 JN 15:9-12
41 JN 15:13

Jesus (the name means "saves") came not to condemn, not to judge, but to save all humankind.[42] That includes you and me. Jesus represents God's plan for our growing into union with the Divine. We call this salvation.

Through members of his Church and by the power of the Holy Spirit, Jesus continues to call us to love, so our joy may be complete.

Finally, Jesus will come again, in full glory, at the end of time. Those who have loved as Jesus taught will be reunited with their glorified bodies in a world made whole. The Kingdom will be complete. This is what we mean when we say, "resurrection of the dead and the life of the world to come." Sounds complicated, but I love the idea.

---

42   JN 3:16

God Leads Us to Love

The Spirit is the breath of life

If Jesus represents the "what" of God's plan for salvation, The Holy Spirit represents the "how." The Spirit is the way God the Father and God the Son live in us.

The Holy Spirit is the living breath of God. All life is sustained by the breath of God, for the foundation for all life is spiritual. Working with the Son, the Spirit gives life. The Holy Spirit helps us live life fully with His gifts: love, joy, peace, patience, kindness, goodness, faithfulness, gentleness, and self-control.[43]

The Spirit enables faith

The Holy Spirit awakens and kindles faith in us.[44] It is through the Holy Spirit that we come to know the Father and the Son. The Holy Spirit spoke through the prophets, inspired Scripture, prepared Mary, and gave birth to the Church at Pentecost. The Holy Spirit is the way we grow spiritually.

Jesus gave us the Holy Spirit to be our advocate.[45] This means the Holy Spirit helps us in our incompleteness. He comforts, frees from sin, heals, nourishes, and intercedes for us in prayer.[46] These graces of the Holy Spirit are the way most of us come to know the unconditional love of God.

The Spirit enables Sacraments

Roman Catholics are often referred to as a sacramental people because Sacraments are important in Roman Catholicism. The Church defines a Sacrament as an efficacious sign of grace, instituted by Christ and entrusted to the Church, by which divine life is dispensed to us through the work of the Holy Spirit.[47] This means Sacraments are living encounters with the Divine. During these encounters, we receive a special gift of God's love called grace.

Sacraments are life-giving powers that come from the Body of Christ through the action of the Holy Spirit.[48]

---

43   Catechism, 736
44   Catechism, 683
45   JN 14:16
46   Catechism, 688
47   Catechism, 774
48   Catechism, 1116

There are seven Sacraments: Baptism, Confirmation, Eucharist, Reconciliation, Anointing of the Sick, Matrimony, and Holy Orders. These seven Sacraments touch all stages and all the important moments of Christian life[49] (Baptism = birth, Eucharist = nourishment, Reconciliation = forgiveness, Confirmation = growth into maturity, Marriage and Holy Orders = life commitments, and Anointing of the Sick = illness and death).

Sacraments are God's gift to help us live life more fully, so we may know the reality of joy.

The Spirit speaks through Prophets

The Holy Spirit is responsible for Divine Inspiration of those people selected by God to understand and proclaim either God's revelation or more personal inspiration. As such, both Sacred Scripture and Tradition are made possible through the action of the Holy Spirit. In the Sacrament of Baptism, we are called to be prophets.

The Spirit leads us to love

The Holy Spirit continues to be present in the Church, guiding it toward its final destination.

The Holy Spirit is God's gift, poured out through Jesus to each one of us and to the entire Church Community. The Holy Spirit will be with us until the end of time, leading us to love. For love is God's plan for salvation.

In the end, all that matters is love.

---

49   Catechism, 1210

Summary

God Is

God is
God is the only God
God is real
God is almighty

God is Love

God is love
Love creates
Love requires choice
Love reveals
Love is relational

God Calls Us to Love

Jesus is the Word
Jesus is God's Word made man
Jesus calls us to love

God Leads Us to Love

The Spirit is the breath of life
The Spirit enables faith
The Spirit enables Sacraments
The Spirit leads us to love

For those of you who are wondering what happened to Mary, the Mass, saints, sin, and all the rest, please be patient. No building is stronger than its foundation. It is only when the basic truths are integrated into a person's life that the other teachings of the Church make sense.

For those of you who finished this chapter and thought, "My God, how am I going to ever make this part of my life?" (I count myself part of this category), I have good news: You have asked the right question.

It is now time to talk about faith.

But don't forget: God is love.

III
The Journey

In Brief

I'm sorry, John.

John is a good friend of mine. We do missions and retreats together, so we spend a lot of time talking about spirituality. Usually, he is very even-handed in his evaluation of my ideas. But when I mentioned to him that I was planning on using the concept of journey to discuss Catholicism, he almost expired. "Over-used" and "simple minded" were, I believe, his kindest words.

So, I'm sorry, John. I still like it. Besides, how can you have "lights along the path" unless the path is going somewhere?

The First Step

Some years ago, my wife, Frannie, and I visited the Holy Land. It was a transforming experience with many wonderful moments. I was surprised, however, by the site that touched me most deeply.

We had just finished visiting Nazareth and were boarding our tour bus. Nazareth is located near the top of a very large hill (in New England we might even call it a mountain). As I sat down in my seat next to a window I happened to look out to the east. Before me was a series of rolling hills, wild and brushy-looking, gently stretching down to the plain below. I think the shore of Lake Genesseret (also known as the Sea of Galilee) was a faint glimmer in the distance, but I may have imagined this.

I started to cry as I thought of Jesus, standing where the bus was standing, trying to take that very first step toward his new life. Matthew's Gospel states simply that after his baptism and time in the desert, "He left Nazareth and made his home in Capernaum by the lake."[50] God, he must have felt lonely. He must have struggled. How did he do it?

The answer may seem obvious: Jesus was divine. He didn't have the concerns you and I might have. This answer, however, doesn't work for me. Jesus was both divine and FULLY human. He had feelings just like us. It would have been a lot easier to stay put, wait until he was better prepared, until he had everything in order.

At some level, he must have known he was leaving everything: family, friends, life as he knew it. He knew his cousin John had been arrested for doing what he was about to start doing. He was setting off to proclaim a new Kingdom. To strangers. By himself.

How did he decide to take that first step?

We will never know for sure, but in my mind, the answer is relatively simple. Jesus had asked himself the right question: What was important, most important, to him? No one can begin a meaningful faith journey without first deciding why the journey is important. This was true for Jesus. It is also true for anyone who wants more from life.

I call this question the "religious" question, because religion makes little sense without it. For most of us, the question starts out as something different than "what's most important to me?" For a few, it may be something like the first question Andrew asked

---

50　MT 4:13

Jesus: "Where are you staying?"[51] More often, the question is more personal: "Is this all there is?", "Isn't there anything more?", or even "Life sucks" (I know this isn't a question, but it certainly implies one). In these questions, as well as countless others like them, the common ingredients are a recognition that something is missing in one's life as currently lived, and a yearning for more. Scripture calls this a restlessness of the soul. Think of it as the Holy Spirit calling.

For many of us, this question surfaces most strongly immediately when life tests us most severely. During such times, we are experiencing what Jesus experienced when he went into the desert for forty days. He did this immediately before beginning his public ministry.

One of our good friends loves to talk about religion and spirituality. He gives me books to read, I give him books to read, and then we talk about them, usually over a meal. I enjoy our time together even though I know the discussions will lead nowhere. The same thing is true of many students I have been privileged to teach. They love the intellectual challenge. It's as if they think they are getting ready for Jesus. But, for whatever reason, they have not been willing or able to ask themselves the *religious question*.

Roman Catholicism teaches what it believes to be the fullness of God's revelation to humankind.[52] I share that belief. However, it makes no difference until one is ready to hear it. A meaningful faith journey cannot begin in earnest until the religious question is asked. The traveler must be willing to leave behind past lifestyles and beliefs, comfortable as they may seem, and replace them with a willingness to change, question, and search for truth. He or she must be willing to leave his or her Nazareth.

If none of this makes any sense to you, the good news is you can stop right here. The rest of this book will be a waste of time. But keep the book somewhere nearby—for the time when, for whatever reason, you wonder, "Is this all there is?"

---

51   JN 1:38
52   Catechism, 66

Faith Is a Journey

We all start from different places when it comes to faith. How we were raised plays a big role, but our age, cultural heritage, natural inquisitiveness, recent life experiences, and I am sure many other elements play a role in determining how we think about things like God.

Starting from different places, we then travel at different speeds. Very few of us experience an immediate awakening of the Spirit. It takes time, effort, and patience, sometimes with others, more often with ourselves. Think of it as forming a new habit. One that will grow and become more life-giving the longer we travel.

Along the way, we encounter different people, different life situations, and different crises. I could go on and on, but I think you get the point. Acquiring faith is a journey, a different journey for each of us.

When I first entered the formation program to become a permanent deacon, I was shocked by how little I knew relative to the other men in the program. Stuff like morning and evening prayer, the names of all the epistles, and a good deal of the terminology being tossed around. I was discouraged and wondered if I should even bother continuing. I had fallen victim to one of the great fictions of the spiritual journey: where *you* are is where *I* should be. The important thing is not where I am at any point in time compared to anyone else. The important thing is knowing I am headed in the right direction.

One related thought: Never confuse familiarity with religious terminology and practices with advanced spirituality. The two can be complementary but are not one and the same. When you don't understand something, ask what it means or why we do it. If the one you ask reacts in a "Well, everyone knows that" way, it usually means he or she doesn't know either. Jesus never said it had to be complicated.

There is a flowerpot on the terrazzo wall just outside our living room. The flowers in it are fascinating. They are closed whenever it is dark. As the first rays of light appear, some seem to turn toward them and begin to open. When the sun has risen, they open themselves fully to its light and warmth. They are beautiful and almost twice the size of those blooms that, for whatever reason, fail to open. Those gradually wither.

While there are many definitions of faith, I like the way Jesus described it: a conscious decision to open oneself to the Divine. He did so in his parables, with the good soil producing bountiful harvests from the word of God.[53] He also referred to it in his healing miracles. When a centurion (a non-Jew and enemy of the Jewish people) sought out Jesus in Capernaum to ask for his help with an ailing servant, Jesus was so impressed with the man's openness to his healing power that he remarked, "'Truly I tell you, in no one in Israel have I found such faith.' And to the Centurion he said, 'Let it be done for you according to your faith.'"[54]

There are many dimensions to faith, but I believe a conscious decision to open one's self to the Divine is the starting point for them all. Think of it as opening yourself to the Spirit of life in order to grow in the Spirit. One starts with a decision, with many questions and doubts. And gradually this decision grows into certainty. Certainty that the Divine is intimately present in our lives, helping us become more. More whole. More holy.

If you are puzzled by this definition of faith, a familiar analogy might help. Think of the first few times you encountered someone who later became very important to you, someone such as your spouse or a very close friend. Didn't you find yourself listening more carefully and sharing more fully BEFORE you were certain this was someone destined to be important to you? As you found yourselves attracted to each other, didn't the process of opening more fully continue as your relationship blossomed? Faith involves the same process. Because faith lets God help us build a meaningful relationship with him.

Faith is a gift. Jesus promised that faith could move mountains, allow us to drive out evil spirits, be healed, and live more fully. Sounds appealing, doesn't it? But it doesn't happen all at once. It's still a journey.

Let me give you an example. Any discussion of Catholicism involves a great deal of time on Jesus. Catholicism teaches Jesus is fully human, fully divine, a member of a Trinitarian God who was present at the birth of Creation, became human to save us, is still with us through the Holy Spirit, and will come again to judge the living and the dead at the end of time. A pretty big mouthful, don't you think?

---

53   MT 4:18
54   MT 8:10,13

What isn't often mentioned is that it took the church four centuries to arrive at that consensus. How's that for a LONG journey? The four Gospel authors had varying ideas of just who Jesus was, and the original twelve apostles struggled mightily with the question. All twelve would have probably been shocked by the previous paragraph. In Mark's Gospel, they never get it. In Matthew's, they sort of understand, but at the Ascension—yes, the Ascension—"they doubted."[55] Obviously, coming to know the real Jesus takes time and effort.

And so I have a suggestion: become an apostle. Wonder, question, search. But never let go of these facts: Jesus is real; God sent him; I will follow him.

You will be surprised by the result.

---

55 MT 28:17

Importance of the Journey

The human person is made up of many things. Let me reduce them to mind, body, and spirit, all interconnected. Like the rest of creation, they are related to each other and either grow or wither together. The simple but profound truth is you can't ignore the spirit and hope to live life fully. I think this is the major reason the average human being realizes only ten percent of his or her ultimate potential. [56]

In fact, a healthy spiritual life is the foundation for a vibrant life. One's body and mind are not enough. Roman Catholicism teaches that the spiritual side of things, often referred to as the soul, is so profoundly united to the rest of the human person that it is the major way in which we have been created in God's image.[57]

The journey to increased spirituality is the most important journey any of us ever undertakes. It certainly has been for me. Of course, as with most things, I learned this the hard way.

I was raised in a loving family with three brothers, a father who was often bigger than life, and an Episcopalian mother who was determined to make good on her promise to raise us Catholic. I attended a parochial school from first through eighth grade. Unlike many, I thrived on the mixture of a loving God, demanding academics, and strict discipline. I will forever be indebted to the caring nuns who instilled in me a deep reverence for the Eucharist. I learned to love the sense of mystery and profound giving.

By my early teens, organized religion was losing its appeal. The call to holiness, saints, and prayer were no match for raging hormones, sports, and all-night poker parties. Jesus just didn't seem relevant. I had discovered a whole new world. One that, with a little luck, could all be mine.

By the time I entered college, every breath I took was directed toward making you think I was special. I knew there was a destination out there and if I just worked hard enough and ran fast enough and said the right things and did the right things and bought the right things, I would reach it. I would be happy. I stretched my mind, I abused my body, I worked hard, I played hard, and every time I thought I had reached my goal, another one appeared. The

---

56 *Seasons of the Heart*, John Powell, SJ, p.197
57 Catechism, 365

race to nowhere had begun. I believe Jesus called it the road to destruction.[58]

I married young, at twenty-two years old. It is one decision I have never regretted. My fiancée, Frannie Vincent, was a nonpracticing Unitarian, about as far from Catholicism as one could get. A very wise priest strongly encouraged us to resolve our religious differences before our wedding. He even went so far as to suggest we try and find a faith tradition other than Catholicism, one where we both would be comfortable. My reaction surprised everyone, especially me. For all intents and purposes I had become a nonpracticing Catholic, but at the same time I couldn't imagine being anything else. I had always rationalized that when the Church became more reasonable, I would come back. Besides, being raised Catholic had helped me understand the basics of morality. I wanted the same for our children. Frannie agreed. As has happened many times since, I think she also recognized something in me I couldn't see in myself.

Very quickly we had our first children, two beautiful girls named Hope and Michele. They arrived thirteen months apart, causing my mother-in-law to observe dryly that I should either rethink the rhythm system or find some other hobby to occupy my spare time. I started going to Mass again. My motivation was simple. I had to impress the kids. And my wife. It was all show. But then interesting things began to happen.

In the first burst of post–Vatican II enthusiasm, a young priest announced a once-a-week evening basketball game for interested male parishioners. It was fun, so much so it didn't really bother me when, at the end of our third session, my new priest friend announced we would all be going to Confession before leaving to drink beer. I had rediscovered the spark of belonging generated by becoming part of a community. I began to take Mass attendance more seriously. The search had begun.

Almost before I knew it, we had added two boys, Bill and Tim, to our two girls. I loved being with our kids, but the demands of my career limited my time with them. Frannie was an excellent mother, often taking on the role of both parents when I was traveling. She was also patient with my compulsive enthusiasms and mood swings when things didn't go as I thought they should. Finally, every time I wanted to move the family to better my career opportunities, she was always ready to leave the familiar for the unfamiliar. Church

---

58 MT 7:13

attendance was frequent, but there was no real involvement. I didn't have time.

When we arrived in Ridgefield, Connecticut, a new pastor at St. Mary's went out of his way to befriend us. Father Charlie made us feel special by inviting us to share his spiritual home. Soon others reached out and made an effort to include us. Almost without our knowing it, the whole idea of Church began to take on new meaning.

Over time, St. Mary's became a very special place for us. Our children attended religious education and received sacraments. Frannie became a member of the choir. I made the mistake of questioning why the annual fair made so little money and soon found myself in charge of the next one. When I spent more on raffle prizes for the coming fair than the Parish had taken in from the prior year's event, Father Charlie started spending more time with me. Fortunately, the fair did very well (what Catholic doesn't like a raffle?), and soon Frannie and I were spending more time with the pastor on a variety of projects. Along the way, we met many wonderful people. One special person was a single mother with significant health issues and two daughters. Jeanne, Chrissy, and Claudie soon became part of our extended family.

Every time we did anything, more came our way. It was fulfilling, and I wanted more. Periodically, a thought would cross my mind: "What if this is the real world, and the one where I spend all week is the distraction." But then I would chuckle, and the thought would disappear.

Eventually, after eighteen years of her own journey, Frannie was baptized during the Easter Vigil in 1982. The church was packed with her many friends (and the two-hour service didn't start until 11:00 PM!). One of our sons was the altar boy, egging on the priest to really douse her when it came time for the actual Baptism. Her Unitarian mother was there and actually joined us at the font for the Baptism, anxiously looking at the church walls to make sure they weren't going to collapse.

St. Mary's was where we held the memorial Mass after my father's death. It was where Hope and Michele, as well as our "heart-adopted" daughters Chrissy and Claudie, were married. It is where we held my Mass of Thanksgiving after my ordination to the permanent diaconate. St. Mary's was special. I think it was where we first learned what the term "Body of Christ" means: ordinary people, from different backgrounds and with different outlooks, sometimes petty, sometimes outright disagreeable, but for the most part united in their willingness to make Christ real to one another. For the first time in my life, I felt as if I had found my home. I now experience the same feeling whenever I enter a Church for Mass.

During this time, I had many wonderful experiences. Two stand out because of their special impact on me.

The first began in a surprising way. An acquaintance I rarely saw approached me with an invitation. A retreat for men called Cursillo was going to be held in the near future. For reasons he couldn't fully explain, he wondered if I might want to go. The retreat was designed for those who wanted more from life. You could have knocked me over with a feather. I didn't even think. I just said, "Yes, I think I would like that."

That weekend had a profound effect on me. I am not sure how to describe it other than it was when I first experienced the Divine. It was no longer a question of trying to think my way into contact with God. For a few precious hours, God was present in a way so intense that I can hardly remember the specific activities of the weekend. I slept little. For the most part I just sat and experienced a peace and joy I had never known before.

During that weekend I met Fr. Gavin. He gave me a gift I will never forget. He helped me realize it was good to be me just the way I was. I didn't have to pretend to be special. I already was. Every time he came near me he would reach out, make eye contact, and say, "Bill, be good to yourself."

The thought had never entered my mind. Could it be possible that God actually loved in a way I could experience? I had been taught God was love, but the idea had always seemed to get lost in all the other teachings. Until that weekend, I had never considered that God's love might be real and tangible and part of life. It had never occurred to me this love we call God might actually be in and with me.

Above all, I was struck by the incredible thought that God wants those he loves to be happy, truly happy.

With a certainty that comes only from actual experience, I suddenly knew, to the core of my being, that God cannot be found. But he will always find those who seek. God cannot be seen until his presence is believed. And then his presence can be seen everywhere. In the caring of my wife, the gift of my children, the beauty of colors, the sound of music, the seeming coincidences that were nudging me toward greater certainty of the Divine.

I left that weekend on fire. I was on a mission. I was going to remake the world. And all I needed was a little help from God. I was going to row AND steer the boat. I just needed God to come along for the ride. To see how well I could do both.

Around the same time, a psychologist told us the best way to relate to our children was to find mutually enjoyable activities. Not what you like and they pretend they like. Or the reverse. Child by child, not all at once. This idea seemed reasonable to me. Until our daughter Michele, whom I had done a miserable job relating to, came and asked if I would help her start a retreat program for teens in Ridgefield. It was called Emmaus and was similar to, although shorter than, Cursillo. She had attended one in a neighboring town and wanted to share it with her friends.

Without thinking, I said, "Sure." Our first action was to have two tee shirts made with the words "Ridgefield Emmaus" printed on them. I had no idea what I had gotten myself into.

I don't think I have ever worked harder in my life. The setbacks were many, the successes few and far between. But within six months, with a big assist from Fr. Gavin and several equally clueless new friends, we were able to run a retreat. Despite the mistakes we made, the retreat was a success. I was delighted for many reasons. My daughter had given me a plaque saying she loved me (I still have it). I had done the one Emmaus I had promised to do. I could now get back to my normal life.

That belief lasted less than one day. Teens started calling to ask when we would begin working on the next Emmaus. I couldn't think of a good way to say no. Besides, Frannie, who always knew I would get things screwed up without her, announced she was going to help. It was while working on an Emmaus retreat a year later that Frannie decide to convert. Jesus had become part of her lived experience.

Over the next four wonderful years I learned many things. God is a God of the unexpected. He calls people using whatever is handy. Regardless of how impossible things look, they have a way of working out when you make the effort and trust. Finally, I learned that God has a great sense of humor.

Probably the most important lesson was the realization that whenever I gave, I received more in return than I had given. I became more. Unfortunately, I failed to learn who was responsible for the growth. I had some crazy notion that it was me. Religion and all that went with it were important to me, but it was just one part of my life, and I kept stuffing it into its own little compartment called "things important to me when I have the time." For you see, I was still running the race.

Rapid advancement in the company I worked for fed my ego like injections of a narcotic, energizing my sense of accomplishment, allowing us to buy more, do more, and be more. But it was getting harder and less rewarding. I was beginning to wonder. The feeling never seemed to last. And the letdowns from even minor disappointments became more devastating. Was it possible that I wasn't as capable as I had thought? Or that I was pursing an empty dream? I was now meeting the executives I had idolized. What I couldn't get over was that they were no happier than I was. They were also running the race.

We all seek. I now wonder how I wasted so much time looking in all the wrong places. How I missed the effect spiritual growth had had on my life. How I missed the reality that only the spiritual journey makes all other journeys possible. I was able to accept this only when there was no option. A bit like "when all else fails, read the directions."

For the longest time I had refused to recognize that part of the problem was my drinking. I claimed I was just being sociable. But my life was becoming grayer, my loved ones more distant, my options fewer. I even started to pray for help.

I could still put up a good front, but I was losing contact with what was real and what wasn't. I repeatedly told myself I was just having a run of bad luck. I felt justified in feeling sorry for myself because I could name all the people who were treating me unfairly. If life would simply cooperate a bit, I'd be fine. Of course, the fact I was drinking the better part of a bottle of vodka a day never entered my head. You see, I am an alcoholic. I just didn't know it at the time.

Alcoholism is a disease, which means when I put alcohol in *my* system, it acts differently than when you put alcohol in your system. Alcoholism is serious business. In my case, alcoholism was killing me. My pancreas was under siege. When warned I would die if I didn't stop drinking, I did what any reasonable alcoholic would do: I changed doctors. Alcoholism is also very powerful. By the time I decided to seek help, I knew, to the core of my being, I had to drink. There was no other alternative. I was hopeless.

I have not had a drink for over twenty-five years. So what happened?

My intent here is not to cover the details of how I got sober. It was just part of my journey, a difficult part for a while, but still just

41

part of my journey. The important point is this: All I really did was decide to let God be God so I could finally be me. Without knowing it at the time, I was finally accepting the spiritual journey as THE foundation for all other journeys.

Kicking and screaming, I joined AA. There I finally was forced to give up. I made a decision to let God run my life. What a relief. I had never realized how energy-consuming it was to think I was in charge. One of the sayings I especially loved was "Running the world is a thirsty business." It finally dawned on me that life rarely happened the way I would like. Life just happened.

I have learned many other things from AA. For example, I learned the incredible value of honest sharing with others. We all have stories because we are all human beings trying to become more complete, and we all have life experiences. When I tell my story to someone else, I can see meaning and connections I would otherwise miss. Think of it as giving and getting more in return. When I hear someone else's story, I know I am not alone, and I am enriched by knowing there's company on the journey.

I have learned that our relationships are the most precious possession we have. How we view ourselves, understand others, and recognize the reality of the Divine are all products of our relationships.

I have learned that miracles still happen. My life today is better than I ever imagined it could be while in an alcoholic haze. I am more alive than I ever dreamed I would be. Without the slightest interest in a drink. Not bad for someone who knew he couldn't survive without booze. And my story was mild compared with others.

I have learned there is good news in most things life hands us, if we just look for it. When people first hear I am an alcoholic, they tend to cringe, almost as if they feel sorry for me. I chuckle, because what I have learned and am still learning from AA is priceless. The same has been true for most of the crises in my life.

Most importantly, I learned the spiritual journey is the most important journey I would ever make.

On the chance I would ever again wonder, God led me to Roger.

A Case Study in Spiritual Living

Several years ago, I spent three weeks with the Missionaries of the Poor in the slums of Kingston, Jamaica. They had constructed shelters there to care for people left to die in the streets. There I met Roger Kerr.

Roger was a resident in his mid-twenties who had multiple birth defects. His head was enlarged, and he had a towel tucked into his shirt to catch the saliva he drooled uncontrollably. He could not speak and uttered guttural sounds in an effort to communicate. He walked with a pronounced limp, having very little use of his right leg and right arm.

Roger was one of the happiest persons I have ever met.

I first became aware of Roger as I was sitting on a low concrete wall with several residents late one afternoon. He approached me carrying a Frisbee in his left hand. He nudged me with the Frisbee, obviously asking if I would throw it to him. He had a big smile on his face. Naturally, I took the Frisbee, and once he had backed up about twenty feet, I tossed it to him. I am still not sure how, but about every third time I tossed him the Frisbee, he would actually catch it. Oh, the look on his face when he did! A big smile and grunt of satisfaction.

Roger never seemed to focus on his limitations. He always seemed to be looking for his next adventure. Sorting through some boxes of donated goods one day, Roger discovered a small harmonica. He worked and worked at producing a note of music, and when he finally did, you could just see the joy in his eyes. He had become a musician.

Roger loved to eat, even though the food struck me as barely edible. Before he did so, however, he always made sure he fed the people who had no arms.

Finally, Roger lived for our worship services. He loved to pray. He knew God was real. He seemed so grateful for all he had been given.

As I left Kingston and was reflecting on my stay there, I realized Jesus had been right. Those who are willing to trust do gain life. The Kingdom is theirs.

The following was the last entry in my Kingston diary:

My prayer is that I can become more like Roger.

Focusing on what I can do
Rather than what I can't
On what I have
Rather than what I lack
On my successes
Rather than my failures
On laughter
Rather than despair
On gratitude
Rather than want
On what might be
Rather than what might not...
...So I can make music.

From Where to Where

With all this talk about journeys, some of you may have wondered where we are supposed to be coming from and where we are trying to go: from where to where. I have wondered the same thing, and answers such as "We are trying to get to heaven" may be good theology but make progress difficult to measure, at least for me. So here's a suggested answer that makes sense to me. I heard it first from a wonderful priest, Father Lon V. Konold, of the Missionary Oblates of Mary Immaculate. It helped me. I hope it does the same for you.

We are coming from a reliance on *our* will. We are trying to go to an acceptance of *God's* will.

The Book of Genesis tells us about the idea of original sin. It occurred when Adam and Eve decided they wanted to become like God.[59] They wanted to see as God sees, to become complete on their own, so they would have greater control over their lives.

This is where we are coming from: our tendency to try and be our own God. To live life based on the fundamental premise that we are the center of our own personal universe and that we are capable of becoming whole on our own. We can make it, whatever "it" is, on our own, because we care more than anyone else about what happens to us and we know better than anyone else what will make us happy. When we try and play God, we are being arrogant. The word "arrogant" means having an exaggerated sense of one's own importance or abilities.[60] A corollary is that the purpose of life is to get all we can based on what we achieve.

If this sounds foreign to you, think of what your first, almost instinctive, reaction is when something unexpected happens in your life. Isn't it some form of "How does this affect me?" Or "Am I better or worse off?" Or "If I just eat the apple, won't I be better off?"

This sin is called original sin because it is the source or origin of all other sin. Yet, it's so embedded in our thinking we rebel at the notion that it's wrong.

God, however, seems fairly clear on the subject. His first of Ten Commandments is "I am the Lord your God, who brought you out of... slavery; you shall have no other gods before me."[61] In Deuteronomy, God goes further in establishing the Great Commandment: "The

---

59   Genesis, 3:5
60   New Oxford American Dictionary
61   Exodus 20:2

Lord is our God, the Lord alone. You shall love the Lord with all your heart, and with all your soul, and with all your might."[62] When asked what the most important commandment was, Jesus said the same thing.

Why?

Imagine for a moment what life would be like if for some reason the sun stopped shining. No, I don't mean like in a song; I mean for real. Obviously, the results would be disastrous. Fortunately, we never consider this possibility because the sun never changes. It is always there, supplying just the right amount of light and warmth needed for us to live.

When we are very young, each of us gradually establishes our own personal sun to deal with the seemingly random, and at times chaotic, nature of life. Almost always we end up with one thing that is more important than anything else. When we are children, this is usually our parents, but as we grow older, it can become almost anything. In most cases this one thing is self. I am the one absolute, the only constant in my life. Everything else is understood or, you might say, revolves around this one center of gravity, some receiving my light and warmth, others remaining in darkness.

This approach is fraught with difficulties for a simple reason: life doesn't work that way. No matter how powerful and successful and bright and lucky a person is, no matter how hard that person tries, no one can control everything and everyone around him or her. Life doesn't cooperate. And when our personal sun doesn't shine the way we would like, the impact on us is almost always harmful. Think how you feel when a good friend disappoints you, a hoped-for success turns to failure, someone or something you value greatly disappears from your life.

I think this is why Jesus was so definite whenever asked about the greatest commandment. Make God the most important thing in your life; make God your center of gravity. It's challenging to do, but God is the only "sun" that will never change. Only God is love complete, always present to provide the warmth and light you need. And the more we rely on this love, the more fulfilling it becomes. Helping us keep failures and success, gains and losses...life in all its joy and its disappointments... in the right perspective. For the point of life is not how much we can get, but how well we handle what we receive.

---

62   Deuteronomy 6:4

This is where we are trying to go: living with God as the center of our universe. In case you wondering, this does not mean spending every moment praying to or thinking about God. While there are some who are called to this lifestyle, the meaning is much simpler: Who's in charge? Jesus summarized the whole idea very well: Your (not my) Kingdom come, your (not my) will be done....

When you accept the fundamental beliefs covered in the Chapter II, "Lights Along the Path," it's really quite simple. Who knows the most? Who knows me best? Who has a better idea of what will lead to my lasting happiness? In the end, who loves me more?

What's at stake? A vibrant spiritual life, which is the path to a more vibrant life in general. Jesus called it eternal life.[63]

In a very real sense, the Bible is a collection of stories about God trying to lead his people out of slavery. Slavery to self and all the other false gods we encounter along the way. At times we fail. At times we are all stiff-necked people, because we are all human. So please remember: Jesus never asked anyone to be perfect, only to make the effort. There is a Promised Land, and God has promised to lead us to it,[64] if and when we let him.

I love the way the Psalms say it: "Bless the Lord." When applied to the way we view God, the word "blessing" means adoration of and surrender to the Creator.[65] Think of adoration as loving with great awe. Think of surrender as unconditional.

I will bless the Lord at all times.
His praise shall continually be in my mouth.
My soul makes its boast in the Lord;
Let the humble hear and be glad.
O magnify the Lord with me,
And let us exalt his name together.
I sought the Lord and he answered me,
And delivered me from all my fears.
Look at him, and be radiant;
So your faces shall never be ashamed.
This poor soul cried, and was heard by the Lord,
And was saved from every trouble.
O taste and see that the Lord is good;
Happy are those who take refuge in him.[66]

---

63 John 3:16
64 Isaiah 54:10, 55:11
65 Catechism, 1078
66 Psalm 34, 1-8

47

The Psalms call us to bless the Lord; to surrender unconditionally. So we may be made whole.

There Are Many Paths

Perhaps my most conclusive AA lesson involved something I think I had always known but had never thought much about: There are many paths to the Divine. A specific religious tradition like Roman Catholicism is only one of them. Anyone who claims otherwise is limiting a God who has no limits. Such behavior belittles God and is a form of idolatry. This applies to different faith traditions as well as different approaches to Roman Catholicism.

Participation in AA is impossible without recognizing the existence of a personal God willing to work miracles in one's life. What makes it interesting is each person is invited to search for the God, or "Higher Power," of his or her understanding. Period. This is the end of the God description. And when one is willing to make the effort, it always—yes, always—works.

I have seen people who, for any number of reasons, refused to acknowledge the possibility of any kind of God. They never got better. I have known men and women so alienated by organized religion and yet so beaten by their addiction that in a gesture of surrender, they pretended there was a God who might help. That's right, pretended. They got better. Always. I have witnessed men and women with no clue what to do make their Higher Power the people they were meeting. They got better. Always. Anyone who sincerely tried to open himself or herself to the power of the Divine in some way got better. Sounds a little like the way Jesus talked about faith, doesn't it?

Once I reflected on what I was observing, I was profoundly moved. For perhaps the first time I understood what the *unconditional* love of God actually meant. I felt as though I could reach out and touch the reality of a God who loves each one of us more than we can imagine. Patiently waiting to be asked into our lives. To help us become more.

This is how Jesus portrayed the Divine. This is how Jesus lived, never refusing to help anyone who made the effort to seek his help.

The really interesting thing is that these same people I referred to earlier continued to grow so long as their image of a personal God continued to grow. So long as they were growing spiritually. When their God stopped becoming more, so did they.

Many of the friends I have made in AA, as well as people I have met elsewhere, make a point of differentiating between spirituality and religion. Their tone of voice almost always implies an inherent goodness in spirituality that is lacking in religion. As I hope you can tell by now, I see little difference in what the two set out to accomplish. Spirituality means accepting there is a power greater than yourself and making a concerted effort to grow into union with that power. Religion has exactly the same goal. The word "religion" comes from Latin words that mean to reconnect.[67] The only valid reason for religion is to help us connect with, and bond more completely with, the Divine and each other.

The actual difference between spirituality and religion seems to lie in whether you prefer a do-it-yourself approach or a more organized effort. I readily admit there is an obvious liability in the more organized approach; other human beings are involved. And whenever humans are involved, mistakes are made. People have disagreements. A certain priest or minister may disappoint you. At times you may feel slighted or even offended.

But there is another side to that coin. Learning to love others as God loves us is easier to do when others are involved. People not of my choosing but just people, with all their needs and wants and joys and fears and idiosyncrasies. All forms of Christianity are based on the notion of a community of believers, helping one another grow spiritually by struggling to do so together.

Whenever I go it alone, I start off great. But I often end up making wrong turns and hitting dead ends I could have avoided if I had had some company traveling with me. When I am on my own I also find it to easier to stop making any forward progress at all and fail to recognize it. But then, I am still a work in process. At least for me, I appreciate all the help I can get.

I like the way Catholicism deals with this whole subject. There are many paths,[68] but there is only one God.[69] Whatever approach you and I may take to the Divine, we are dealing with the same God.

This one God includes Jesus and the Holy Spirit. So however we may want to deal with this God, we end up dealing with the same Jesus[70] and the same Holy Spirit.[71] Jesus and the Holy Spirit are the ways God interacts with his creation, even when we fail to recognize

---

67   *Deacon Digest,* July, 2011, p. 21
68   Catechism, 819, 847, 1260
69   Catechism, 200
70   Catechism, 819
71   Catechism, 1260

it. Remember: God's love has no limits, accepting us however we come to him.

This one God desires the salvation (think of salvation as complete unity with the Divine) of all humanity.[72] Salvation comes from God alone.[73] As such, salvation is available to everyone who seeks God with a sincere heart and makes the effort to live in accord with his will through the dictates of his or her conscience.[74] It's a question of being willing to make the effort. Said another way, effort is not optional. This also makes sense to me. Love involves choice, and the choice to love takes effort. When we are willing to do so, God's love will take care of the rest.

Catholicism also teaches that the "fullness of the means of salvation" is available in the Catholic Church.[75] This does not mean today's non-Catholics only get a second rate salvation. What it does mean is Catholics are exposed to the fullness of what God has publicly revealed. It may be my upbringing, or maybe I'm just a sucker for what I see as better odds, but I believe this to be true.

An example might help.

Roman Catholics are taught that Christ is truly present, "body and blood, soul and divinity"[76] in the form of bread and wine consecrated at the Mass. When it is consumed, believers grow in communion, or union with the Divine and one another. In our view, God revealed this truth in the Old Testament, the Gospels, and the letters of Paul as well as through the experience of early Christians. The original apostles and their successors, under the guidance of the Holy Spirit, have ensured this revelation remain intact over the centuries.

More on the Eucharist later. The important point now is that this is an example of what is meant by the "fullness of the means of salvation."

Unfortunately, some have chosen to interpret the belief in the fullness of the means of salvation as a reason for exclusivity. This is wrong and is particularly so when preached by Catholics. God is not exclusive. Fullness of the means of salvation should be understood for what it does and does not mean. The fullness of the means of salvation does not mean salvation is possible only through the Catholic Church. It does mean a body of beliefs the Catholic Church

---

72   Catechism, 851
73   Catechism, 169, 620
74   Catechism, 847
75   Catechism, 816
76   Catechism, 1374

teaches has its origin in God and is available to anyone willing to "listen to or hear in faith."[77] It also means members of the Church should be an embodiment of Christ's love in helping each other come to a deeper understanding of how to live life more fully. To remember they are part of the living Body of Christ.[78]

The Church also teaches that every member is called to continued renewal, meaning a willingness to try and become more like Christ to one another. We do this by making the effort to accept and understand one another, to work and pray together, to walk the walk together with members of our own community and every community with which we come in contact. So that, over time, all will come to know that while there may be many paths, there is truly only one God.[79]

---

77 Catechism, 144
78 Catechism, 791
79 Catechism, 821

Summary

The first step

The first step of the spiritual journey involves asking the religious question, which is always some expression of the desire for greater fulfillment in life.

Faith is a journey

We are all at different points in the journey to increased spirituality. The important thing is not where we are in relation to others but whether we are headed in the right direction. Faith is a conscious willingness to open ourselves to the Divine. Growth in faith occurs over time, starting with a decision, with many questions and doubts, and gradually growing into certainty. Faith is a great gift.

Importance of the journey

The faith journey is the most important journey we ever undertake. Healthy spirituality is the foundation for a healthy and vibrant life.

A case study in spiritual living

Roger Kerr is a case study in the advantages of a healthy spiritual life.

From where to where

The spiritual journey is a journey from reliance on our will to seeking God's will for us.

There are many paths

There are many paths to the Divine. Organized religion, and Roman Catholicism specifically, are not the only paths. Claiming exclusive access to the Divine belittles God and is a form of idolatry. The goals of spirituality and organized religion are the same. The difference lies in making the journey on our own versus doing so in conjunction with others. Catholicism teaches that salvation is available to all who seek God with a sincere heart and live in accord with his will through the dictates of their conscience. All those seeking the Divine are dealing with the one true God. The fullness of the means for salvation is available in the Catholic Church.

IV
Rules of the Road

In Brief

What follows are lessons I have learned along the way, often through my own missteps or those of loved ones who travelled with me. They are not official Roman Catholic doctrine except where noted. In my opinion, all are consistent with the teachings of the Church. Besides, what's a book on Catholicism without some rules?

Every trip is made easier if the traveler understands the things he cannot change that affect his journey: the rules of the road. Such as what side of the road to travel on, what the various road signs mean, the hazards to avoid, and what the potential costs will be. The faith journey is the same, the primary difference being the journey gets easier and the rules of the road simpler the farther you go.

Ready vs. Willing

The first rule involves a decision: Are we willing to make the trip? It's senseless to start without being committed to the journey.

In first-century Israel, a man wanting to become a rabbi would start selecting followers when he was around thirty years old. Prior to that he dedicated his life to a study of the Scriptures. This started at a very early age and involved a process that gradually culled out all but the most gifted scholars. A new rabbi was judged by the quality of the scholars he chose to become his followers. These followers became known as learners or disciples because they wanted to learn their rabbi's interpretation of Scripture.

Imagine the surprise when Jesus chose his disciples. Not a single one, with the possible exception of Judas, had any formal training. They all came from very ordinary backgrounds. Once more, with the exception of John's Gospel they were not invited, they were called. Called to walk and talk and live with him: to become part of his way. They left everything to do just that. Not because they were ready, but because they were willing.

God rarely calls the ready. The Apostles weren't ready, Mary wasn't ready, Joseph wasn't ready, most of the Prophets weren't ready, David wasn't ready, Moses wasn't ready, Abraham wasn't ready. The only thing they all had in common was that they were willing.

Approximately ten years ago, my Parish in New Hampshire was twinned with another Parish because of the priest shortage. The new pastor (who resided in the other Parish) asked a pleasant and eminently qualified woman named Mary Sullivan to become our Parish Administrator. Near seventy at the time, she had to move to a new house (our Parish rectory) in a new town to take on new responsibilities. She was greeted with cool disdain from parishioners who wondered why WE didn't have the resident priest. She had to endure snubs from a Diocesan staff that couldn't seem to accept a woman as the person responsible for a Parish.

Today, the Parish continues to serve the needs of all who come to be fed. Whenever I see Mary there is smile on her face and love in her heart. Mary has made the effort, and left the results to God.

So, don't worry about whether you are adequately prepared. You will probably never be. The important question is this: Are you willing? To walk and talk and live with him? To make the effort?

Even when making the effort isn't the obvious, easy, or comfortable thing to do?

Life Happens

Being willing is important because life happens.

At weddings I have had the privilege to witness, I often forecast the future for the newly married couple. It's a fun way to get people's attention and easy to do. My forecast is always the same: Whatever you think is going to happen probably won't. Things you haven't dreamt of will. Life is going to turn out differently than what you think or are hoping it will.

When I then encounter these same couples years after their wedding, one of their first questions is how I knew. Never once have couples told me life happened the way they thought it would. The answer is simple, if a bit perplexing. Life happens.

This is hard for some to accept. And so we tend to attribute random occurrences in our lives to luck, the will of God, or the actions of another. But whatever the cause, life still happens. To the most and the least gifted, the most and least affluent, the most and the least spiritual. There will be times of triumph and times of failure, joy and disappointment, well-being and suffering. Sometimes when we expect them, often when we don't. Think of it as a rule of the road.

While God knows all things and has a plan for his creation, we are not privy to it. We are faced with what appears to be the unpredictability of life. This has led some to conclude life is a period of testing. We are expected to endure difficulties and hardship in the hope of ill-defined future happiness in what we call heaven. Faith becomes a means to endure suffering and adversity; religion is a way to comfort ourselves on this long road.

Some of Jesus' teachings seem to support this line of reasoning, including the Beatitudes (Blessed are the poor, those who mourn, the hungry and thirsty, the persecuted)[80] and calls to love enemies,[81] take up your cross, and lose one's life.[82] Jesus asks us to all this for the sake of the Gospel.

Many early Christians were faced with suffering, persecution, and even death at the time the Gospels were written. This is one of the reasons the first three Gospels emphasize Jesus' teachings on perseverance in the face of calamities. There still are missionary Christians who face deprivation and danger. There are also countless

---

80   MT 5:3,4,6,10

81   MT 5:44

82   MT 10:39

well-intended priests and other ordained ministers who deal with loneliness, a lack of supportive friendships, and the never-ending demands to be present to others. All for the sake of the Gospel.

Having said all this, here is my response: To conclude that religion is a form of medication meant to anesthetize us to the trials of life misses the whole point of what Jesus was trying to accomplish.

Medication is not good news. I give Jesus credit for being smart enough to know that.

Jesus came to proclaim the good news of his Father's Kingdom of love: a Kingdom he claimed was in the process of being realized. Brought to fulfillment in the future but available in the present. He taught, listened, healed and loved. He helped people see the goodness in themselves. He even died so that we might live life more fully.

He consistently used images of celebration in his parables and teachings. When asked why his disciples were not fasting, Jesus said, "The wedding guests cannot fast while the bridegroom is with them, can they? So long as they have the bridegroom with them, they cannot fast."[83] Whenever I read this passage, I wonder whether most Christians know Jesus promised to be with us always.

Christianity is meant to be a religion of celebration. We celebrate the good news. We celebrate that God is real, created us in love, dwells within us, and will lead us to love.

One of my dreams is to have Catholics who come to Mass only on Easter and Christmas see the value in coming all the time. How could that happen? Imagine everyone who attended Mass regularly living life with a sense of joy. Yes, everyone, with a ready smile and an eagerness to reach out to others in a spirit of friendship. Think of the power of attraction. The power of invitation rather than obligation. The power of good news.

So why all the references to the trials of life in Scripture? For most of us, the answer is simple: life happens.

One of the more common misunderstandings I encounter in people seeking a closer relationship with the Divine is the belief God will protect them from life. This is not true. God never promised an absence of storms, assurance of success, or even good health. He did not promise to change life.

What he did promise was to help us change. So we would know serenity in the midst of storms, gratitude for our successes, and hope in the face of our most difficult moments. Roger Kerr and his Frisbee ARE a reality.

---

83   MK 2:19

He also promised to bring good from whatever happens to us if we are willing to trust in his love, to trust even when understanding fails. To be willing to live life rather than be buried by it; to take up our crosses, whatever they may be, and follow him.

Effort vs. Results

Accepting that life has its ups and downs does not mean we must passively accept what comes our way. As I hope has become clear by now, we are still responsible for making the effort. This includes discerning what's important, making choices, planning for the future, and setting goals. Doing our best. However, one of the hardest rules to implement is to avoid the expectation of specific results. We are responsible for the effort, not the results. Think of it as rowing the boat and leaving the steering to God. This is true for everyone, but particularly so for those of us involved in any form of ministry.

Jesus made a point of calling people to account. At times, he made people so uncomfortable they were forced to decide what was important to them and then act based on their conclusions. To make the effort based on what they thought best. However, he never asked anyone to achieve a specific result.

With the exception of religious leaders whose behavior he was criticizing, Jesus almost never answered a question. He would ask another question or tell a story. When a lawyer asked who his neighbor was, Jesus told the parable of the Good Samaritan and then asked his questioner, "Which of these three, do you think, was a neighbor to the man who fell into the hands of the robbers?"[84] Notice: Jesus did not answer the question but turned it around so the lawyer had to think and then declare himself.

Jesus told stories and asked questions to engage his listeners. To help them discern the truth and to take responsibility for their actions. Yet, he *never* asked anyone to achieve a specific result.

Let us return for a moment to the story of the Good Samaritan. After a priest and a Levite fail to help a stricken traveler, a Samaritan (considered a foreigner by Jews) does. He bandages the afflicted traveler's wounds and then takes him to the next inn. Once there, he pays the innkeeper to care for the ailing man, promising to pay for any additional costs when he returns. And then he leaves. He has made the effort.

When Peter encounters Jesus on the shores of Lake Genesseret after his resurrection, Jesus does not criticize him for his earlier denial. He does not demand anything. He simply asks, "Do you love

---

84   LK: 10:36

me?",[85] not once but three times. And each time he responds to Peter's affirmative answer with "Feed my sheep." [86] Make the effort.

Jesus follows a similar pattern in the instructions he gives seventy disciples when sending them out to heal and proclaim the good news. When people refuse to welcome them and their message, "Go out in the streets and say, 'Even the dust of your town that clings to our feet, we wipe off in protest against you. Yet know the Kingdom of God has come near. I tell you, on that day it will be more tolerable for Sodom than for that town.'"[87] Make the effort; leave the results to God. Jesus never asked anyone to achieve results; he always called the willing to make the effort.

Hard as it may seem to those of us raised in a "you can accomplish anything" culture, there is a wonderful logic behind this rule. When we base our lives on results, we are setting ourselves up for failure. Why? Because specific results are often beyond our control, and failure to meet specific expectations almost always reduces our happiness.

Interestingly, the reverse is also true: Exceeding very low expectations almost always increases our sense of happiness. This means that God, to a large extent, has given us the ability to control our happiness. We can determine how we feel about ourselves, others, and even our God. What a great gift! We have only one person to worry about, so to speak.

But if I do everything God wants me to do, why won't he just do what I want him to, when what I want seems so obvious to me?

One of my biggest surprises in studying Scripture was startlingly simple: God is a God of the unexpected. Throughout Biblical history, he has seldom done the obvious.

Think how Abram (later Abraham), the equivalent of a homeless Bedouin, felt when some strange voice promised to make him the father of many nations. Why didn't God pick someone from one of the prosperous kingdoms nearby?

The same question can be asked about God selecting the Jews, a loosely knit group of tribes who owned nothing, or David, the youngest and least obvious son. Imagine how Zechariah felt when informed by an angel that his aging wife was pregnant. Or Joseph when told his fiancée was pregnant. Not to mention Mary's surprise at the same announcement.

---

85   JN 21:15
86   JN 21:17
87   LK 10:11-12

Most Jews do not recognize Jesus as the Messiah because he was raised in the remote, predominantly non-Jewish area of Galilee; proclaimed a Kingdom different from what they wanted; and died in a way they had never imagined. They refuse to change because he was not what they had expected, based on preconceived notions of how God should act. Sometimes I fear we may fail to recognize Jesus when he comes again, whether to us personally or the world at large, for the same reason.

I could go on, but I think you can see the point. God is God and will act in the way he sees fit. For our good and the good of all his creation. The fact he does so in what we see as unexpected ways may say more about the wisdom of our judgments than the wisdom of his.

When I was first ordained, I was assigned to my home Parish in Ridgefield, Connecticut. I was comfortable working with young people in the Parish and assisting at various liturgical functions. I looked forward to a long career in that one Parish. The only thing I knew for sure is I would be uncomfortable dealing with the elderly and dying.

I now split my time between three Parishes, two in New Hampshire and one in Florida (you can probably guess where we spend which parts of the year). My ministry is quite varied. The most rewarding parts involve dealing with the elderly and dying. I have never been happier.

Where God leads us may be different from what we think we want or need. He may do so on a schedule different from ours. But, when given the opportunity, God will always lead us to greater fulfillment. Not what we expected. Better. That's the promise. The Promised Land.

So long as we are willing to make the effort.

Moral Conscience

I had a good chuckle recently while reading an opinion piece by *New York Times* columnist David Brooks. In it, he was wondering how organized religion would react to mounting evidence that the desire to do the right thing is programmed into our genes. Of all the potential reactions he postulated, he missed the one I thought most obvious.

You see, for centuries the Catholic Church has taught that human beings have embedded within them a capability to discern right from wrong, along with a natural inclination to do so. Our terminology may not include terms like genes and genetic makeup, but the result is the same. We call this capacity moral conscience.

We all have a conscience. It is at the core of free will, for it is allows us to make judgments about our actions.[88,] Residing within our conscience is a predisposition to do good and avoid evil.[89] Think of this predisposition as a set of embedded laws, sort of like the Ten Commandments made perfect by Jesus' teachings. Right is right because right is right. Wrong is wrong for the same reason. These "laws" are not Church laws. They represent the way we have been created.

Some time ago, Steven Pinker wrote an article called "The Moral Instinct" for the *New York Times Magazine.* In it he talked very knowledgably about the presence of inherent morality within humankind. I mention his article because Pinker emphasized the need to develop the inherent capability to discern right from wrong and the risks associated with not doing so. Once again, the Church teaches the same thing.

Every human being is responsible for developing the gift of conscience. We call this formation of conscience, and it is a lifelong responsibility.[90] We form or educate our conscience through lived experience, education (including assimilation of Holy Scripture and Church Tradition), familiarity with Church moral teaching, our search for God and truth, faith, and prayer. By making the effort. It is hard to overemphasize the importance of this responsibility for a very significant reason.

With a properly formed conscience, "Man has the right to act in conscience and in freedom to make moral decisions. He must

---

88   Catechism, 1749, 1778
89   Catechism, 1776
90   Catechism, 1783, 1784

not be forced to act contrary to his conscience. Nor must he be prevented from acting according to his conscience, especially in religious matters."[91] "In all he says and does, man is obliged to follow faithfully what he knows to be just and right."[92]

I have used the Catechism to make these points because most Catholics are surprised to realize the Church teaches we must live by the dictates of a formed conscience. The Catholic Church tells us we must think for ourselves. We are responsible for deciding what is right and wrong. And then living by—and in the end being judged by—our decisions. This is the way it must be. We are called to love, and our destiny is love. Love is not love without choice.

Sometimes it is difficult to know the right course of action. While it would be convenient if right were always white and wrong always black, unfortunately, life includes many shades of gray. I have found Church teaching to be helpful when this happens. If particular, the Church suggests three rules that apply in all cases:

1. One may never do evil so that good may result from it. The end does not justify the means.
2. Remember the Golden Rule: Do onto others as you would have them do to you.
3. Respect others and their right to follow their conscience. Do nothing that harms either.[93]

Imagine what the world would be like if all who claim to be Christians, or just those who are active Roman Catholics, or even just those involved in formal Church ministry, followed these rules! Just imagine. I think the world we live in would be transformed.

A well-developed conscience "guarantees freedom and engenders peace of heart."[94] Why? Because, in a sense, God speaks to us through our conscience.[95]

The more developed our conscience, the better we will hear him. To help us with questions like "How do I know the will of God for me?" and "I'm willing to make the effort, but what do I do next?"

Have you noticed we almost always justify what we are about to do by deciding it will bring good? But then, after taking a specific

---

91   Catechism, 1782
92   Catechism, 1778
93   Catechism, 1789
94   Catechism, 1784
95   Catechism, 1776

action, we feel a sense of being either worse or better off. We feel as though we have either lost or gained. That's conscience.

Many years ago, I loved to buy cars. One day I actually bought two while out grocery shopping. I convinced myself I was doing it to make it easier for my family. My wife's reaction left little doubt about the quality of my decision-making. I may have gained two new cars, but I immediately knew I had lost a lot more.

When I was drinking, I knew it was wrong but still could convince myself some good would be accomplished: I would feel better. But then, afterwards, the feeling of remorse would be almost overwhelming. There was no question I had lost a part of my life.

When I take the time to listen to another's story, or reach out to comfort someone in pain, or help someone in need, even at the cost of delaying whatever important things I was supposed to be doing, I feel better afterwards. I feel as though I am more. Always. Often I can't even remember those supposedly important things I had planned to do.

The first time I heard about the permanent diaconate, I was sitting in church with my wife. At the end of Mass, the priest announced that the Diocese was taking applications for a new class of permanent deacons. I turned to my wife and said something like "That's what I want to do." Quite reasonably, Frannie asked, "What's a permanent deacon?" My response? "I don't have the foggiest idea. But that's what I am going to do." By now, you can understand why Frannie is so special. She just smiled.

It took a while for her to get comfortable with the idea and for me to learn what it was I was so sure I wanted to do. But six years later, I entered the formation program for the permanent diaconate.

When we pay attention to our conscience, we gradually develop the ability to avoid experiences that suck life from us and to spend more time on experiences that are life-giving. We find it easier to be willing when the right opportunities appear (particularly the unexpected ones) and increasingly wary of opportunities involving the big "Me" trying to take charge.

Remember my friend Fr. Gavin? He has a wonderful way of describing it. A gymnast must be willing to practice, and then practice some more, if he or she wants to become more grace-ful. We must also, if we want to become more grace-filled. So that, in fact, we will increasingly recognize the voice of God in our lives, and the true freedom and peace of heart that voice brings.

Seeking Truth

In John's Gospel, Jesus has an interesting exchange with Pilate just prior to being condemned to death. In response to Pilate's question, "So you are a King?" Jesus responds," You say that I am King. For this I was born, and for this I came into the world, to testify to the truth. Everyone who belongs to the truth listens to my voice."[96] To which Pilate responds, "What is truth?"[97]

What is truth?

Throughout recorded history, humankind has struggled to understand truth. That is not always as easy as it would seem. But for our purposes, let us define truth as that which is in accord with reality. Truth is reality, what is real.[98] The Catholic Church teaches that God is truth;[99] that the Creed is a summary of the principal truths of our faith;[100] that Jesus is the way, the life, and the truth;[101] and that the Holy Spirit will lead us to truth.[102] That's a lot of truth bouncing around. And therein lies the risk.

When we are exposed to religious teachings, particularly at a young age, there is a tendency to treat them as the only truths. As we mature and are exposed to other truths, some of which seem to contradict our religious training, we have a problem. This often leads to an "either/or" kind of debate. The losers in this debate? Everyone involved.

Jesus had a simple answer: I am the truth.[103] When you find truth you have found me. The Word of God, revealing the reality of the Divine. This is a critically important point, or rule if you would like, for our spiritual journey. An unwillingness to seek truth in favor of unquestioning adherence to currently held beliefs diminishes the grandeur of God and stifles the growth of moral conscience. Growth in any form requires change, and Jesus clearly calls us all to a lifelong willingness to change.

Adapting our beliefs to incorporate new truths requires flexibility. Rob Bell, founding pastor of the Mars Hill Church in Grandville, Michigan, uses a wonderful simile in his book *Velvet Elvis*. He

96   JN 18:37
97   JN 18:38
98   New Oxford American Dictionary
99   Catechism, 144
100   Catechism, 187
101   Catechism, 2614
102   Catechism, 243
103   JN 14:6

compares the spiritual journey to jumping on a trampoline. The springs of the trampoline are our beliefs. The springs are not the reason for trampoline. They are what make the trampoline work. Our beliefs, as constituted at any point in time, are not the journey. They are not the Divine. They make the journey to the Divine work. For this to happen, these "springs" must be flexible, allowing us to jump ever higher as we grow in our understanding of how to use them.[104]

Since its inception, the Catholic Church has taught that the Bible is true. However, the definition of truth has evolved, albeit slowly, over time. For many centuries the Church held that the story of creation, including Adam and Eve, was literally true. The Church now teaches that the story is figurative[105] yet still conveys great truth.

To borrow another metaphor from Rob Bell, when we refuse to allow our beliefs to evolve, as in insisting on a literal interpretation of Genesis, we turn our beliefs into a wall of bricks, with no flexibility. When you pull one brick out, the whole wall begins to crumble.[106] We also tend to confine God to a universe of our understanding.

The alternative seems so simple, and so exciting. Seek the truth. Seek the Lord so he may be found.

Think of the "truths' in the story of creation: God is, God is the source of all, God creates in love, there is an order and goodness in creation, we were created in love, we have free will, sin has a root or original cause, God forgives, and we are called to salvation.[107] The story of Adam and Eve is the story of humankind, and it is our story.

When I view the story from this perspective, my reaction is one of amazement. How did the original authors come up with such a profound way of communicating extraordinarily complex concepts over three thousand years ago? No wonder we believe Scripture is divinely inspired.

Figurative stories or symbolic images can reveal great truths, and they are often the best way to communicate essential truths. Jesus used many figurative stories called parables. It made it easier for his listeners to comprehend and internalize the underlying truths. When we call God "Father" we are using a symbolic image, because we are

---

104   *Velvet Elvis,* Rob Bell, *p. 22*
105   Catechism, 390
106   *Velvet Elvis,* Rob Bell, p.26
107   Catechism, 289

unable to comprehend God fully. The use of figurative or symbolic language is often the only way to convey the greatest truths.

But, you might ask, what about evolution? Doesn't it invalidate Genesis? Answer: it depends. Are we dealing with springs or bricks? If bricks, get ready for endless debates that lead nowhere. If springs, seek and you will find. Seek the truth, but do it with the eyes of faith. And you will find the majesty of the Divine. On the faith journey there need never be a conflict between faith and reason.[108] Both are God-given gifts.

If you aren't sure where to seek concerning evolution, I recommend you read Kenneth Miller's fine book *Finding Darwin's God*. It helped me understand how the warring factions in the debate over evolution have succeeded only in creating intellectual problems for themselves. It also increased my sense of reverence and awe for a Creator who combined ongoing creation and free will in such an ingenious way, which we call evolution. At some level deep within me, I feel closer to the Divine.

Here is one other story about truth that I would like to share with you.

One afternoon, Jesus tells his apostles they are going to take a trip across Lake Genesseret. While this is not mentioned, I suspect the apostles are a little nervous because afternoon storms are common on the lake.

Off they go, and sure enough, a storm comes up. When the apostles look to their leader for guidance, there he is, peacefully asleep in the rear of the boat. Now they get seriously upset and wake him with the admonishing question, "Teacher, do you not care that we are perishing?"[109] Jesus looks around (probably stretches and yawns) and then quiets the storm. He then says, "Why are you afraid? Have you still no faith?"[110] The apostles are impressed but sort of miss the whole point.

I have witnessed a number of discussions concerning this story, which appears in the first three Gospels (Mark, Matthew, and Luke). The question being debated is whether the story is "true," meaning did it actually take place. From my perspective, the debate is a waste of time and energy. There is no way of proving or disproving whether the event literally took place. At the same time, I know I have had times in my life when I have been afraid, often when experiencing

---

108   Catechism, 156-159
109   MK 4:38
110   MK 4:40

70

something out of the ordinary. I have wondered in my heart, "Where are you, God? Are you asleep?" I have also had times when I have been willing to trust in the presence of the Divine, even in the midst of stormy moments, and in those times I have known great calm. I know truth when I see it, even though, like the apostles, I often quickly forget it.

When we are willing to seek the truth, we will often find ourselves filled with truth's cousin, doubt.

I grew up thinking doubt was bad. To question was bad, for it meant I was being unfaithful. I have since learned doubt can be a valuable contributor to spiritual growth. It is not the opposite of faith. Fear is. Faith involves opening ourselves to the Divine, to life—to the truth. Fear does just the opposite, shutting us off from all that is important to us, holding us captive in a self-made prison.

When we want to increase our physical well-being, we walk, we lift weights, we exercise. Doubt is a way of exercising our minds to increase our spiritual well-being. As with physical exercise, it does us no good just to think about it. We must make the effort to do something: like ask questions, read, listen, and pray.

One of the most important ideas of Roman Catholicism is embodied in the Eucharist: that Christ is present, body and blood, soul and divinity, in the consecrated bread and wine. Like many others, I have spent countless hours wondering whether this is true. Asking questions, reading, listening, and praying. The result is a stronger, deeper appreciation of the Eucharist, part of which you will find in the section titled "Real Presence."

In your faith journey, don't ever shy away from truth. Seek the truth. It will help set you free.[111] For everyone who "seeks the truth and does the will of God in accordance with his understanding of it, can be saved."[112]

---

111   JN 8:32
112   Catechism, 1260

Mysteries

Organized religion, and Catholicism in particular, have a whole bunch of mysteries. Like God, the Trinity, the Eucharist, and on and on. Do these mysteries make the search for truth more difficult?

Mysteries used to bother me. When someone said something like "The Trinity is a mystery," my reaction was always the same. I wondered why someone hadn't figured it out. Like they did on TV mysteries. Then we wouldn't have to sit around and wonder why no one had.

I have come to learn there is a different kind of mystery: truths that can be known but never understood. The longer I live, the more I realize that many of the greatest truths in life—like love, and suffering, and God, and my wife—fall into this category. We can know their existence from what we have experienced, like the truth of Jesus calming the storm. We can know them well, but they are beyond our ability to fully comprehend.

A wonderful priest I met on retreat had a useful example. With a wry smile on his face, he said that on some mornings he would look in the mirror and marvel at the mystery he was looking at. There are many mysteries in life.

For those of you who still aren't sure, try to describe love. Try to prove it. Pretty hard to do, isn't it? It can't be touched or seen. Every definition seems incomplete. Yet, anyone who has experienced love has no need for definitions or proof.

Any description of God involves mystery. This is the case because we are the created, not the Creator. Scripture makes it clear that God is infinitely beyond our ability to comprehend, or even imagine. All efforts to do so tend to limit the limitless nature of the Divine. This is why I say God is bigger than any one religion, any one set of words, any one notion of the Divine defined by language, which in and of itself is limiting. Beware of anyone who claims to understand God. Usually that person is creating God in his or her own image and likeness. Personally, I like the fact that God is more complete than I am. It gives me hope.

This is one of the main reasons we use so many symbols, metaphors, and figurative stories in our dealings with the Divine. They are the best, and often the only, way we can come to know that which can never be understood.

But, you might wonder, just how do we come to know the Divine and the truth of other related mysteries? The answer can be found in a discussion of belief.

Believe and You Will See

One of the pivotal stories in the Gospel of Mark occurs more than half way through it. The Apostles just can't seem to get it. They are missing the significance of who Jesus is, despite being with him, listening to his teachings, witnessing his miracles. So Jesus decides to teach them about the nature of belief by healing a blind beggar named Bartimaeus.

As Jesus enters Jericho, Bartimaeus is sitting by the road and begins to shout at him. Warned by others to be quiet, he yells all the louder. Jesus hears the yelling and stops, calling for Bartimaeus to be brought to him. When Jesus asks him what he desires, Bartimaeus says he wants to see. Jesus restores his eyesight and Bartimaeus becomes a disciple of the Jesus he can now see.[113]

Mark uses the story to contrast Bartimaeus' willingness to believe before being able to see with the inability or unwillingness of the apostles to do the same. It seems that belief in Jesus calls for a new way of looking at things.

Most of us decide whether or not to believe something based on the evidence presented to us. Like Thomas, we want to see before we believe. Jesus taught that when it comes to the Divine, or any of the great mysteries, we have to believe to be able to see. We have to become like Bartimaeus.

Another story from Mark might help make this point.

As Jesus is making his way to Jerusalem, some people want Jesus to bless their children. The apostles, seeking to protect Jesus, try to prevent them. Jesus admonishes the apostles, saying, "Let the children come to me; do not stop them; for it is to such as these that the Kingdom of God belongs." [114] I can just see him smile at the children as he beckons them to come forward. But then the smile vanishes, and he turns to the adults: "Truly I tell you, whoever does not receive the Kingdom of heaven of God as a little child will never enter it."[115] Pause. The smile returns, and Jesus takes the children in his arms, laying his hands on them and blessing them.[116]

How do young children come to believe? Believe in anything? The answer lies in their willingness to trust their parents. Based on trust, they believe what their parents tell them. Before they have

---

113   MK: 46-52
114   MK 10:14
115   MK 10:15
116   MK: 10:16

any experience. And then let their life experiences reinforce or force them to reject what they have chosen to believe. Jesus asks us to do the same.

Belief becomes a process of deciding to believe based on trust. Trust in what? For starters, how about the "Lights Along the Path." Trust that God actually chose to reveal them to us. If that's too complicated, trust there is God, he is a God of love, and, in love, sent Jesus to help us. Belief becomes a decision. A decision that is then reinforced or rejected by what we experience.

This is why our lived experience is so important. It is the way we come to *know* the reality of life's greatest mysteries. But it doesn't work without a decision first. Believe, and then you will see.

For those of you who aren't used to this whole trust business and can't quite bring yourselves to try, I would like to propose an exercise. I'm told it's comes originally from the Jesuits, but I like to call it the "Why Not?" formula. Here goes.

Let's say I decide to go through life trusting in a God of goodness and love. I feel better, I grow as an individual, and I live life more fully. And then, when I die it turns out God never existed. What have I lost?

On the other hand, let's say I go through life rejecting the notion of a God of goodness and love. I trust only in myself and what I can see, feel, and touch. I try hard, know momentary pleasures, but, in the end, decide that's all there is to life. And then, when I die, I discover there really is a God of goodness and love.

What have I lost?

If your answer is "nothing" and "a lot," respectively, then "Why Not?"

If, at this point, you are still unwilling to attempt believing as Jesus asks us to do, then I leave you with one of my favorite quotations from Herbert Spencer:

"There is a principle which is a bar against all information, which is proof against all arguments and which cannot fail to keep a man in everlasting ignorance—that principle is contempt prior to investigation."[117]

For those willing to travel this path, my only word of caution is one of patience. Remember: God is a God of the unexpected. He never promised to act on our schedule or in the way we would like. He only promised he would act. Think of it as forming a habit. The habit of faith.

117   Herbert Spencer

A Gospel passage from John illustrates the point beautifully. Jesus gives a man blind from birth his physical sight. When his neighbors ask who was responsible for the miracle, the man's first response is "The man called Jesus." When ridiculed by the religious leaders and pressed by those around him, he thinks about it some more and then responds "A prophet." Finally, he can take no more. Besieged by the disbelief and criticism of the religious leaders, he blurts out, "One thing I do know, that I was blind and now I can see. Do you also want to become his disciples?" He is thrown out for standing his ground (did I mention the journey isn't always pleasant?). But then Jesus reappears and asks him if he believes in the Son of Man. "Who is he, sir? Tell me so that I may believe." Jesus says to him, "You have seen him. You are speaking to him." He says, "I believe." And he falls down and worships him.[118]

Faith is a journey. Believe and you will see.

---

118   JN 9:1-38

Grace

Now, let me see. I've got to accept the fact that life often happens in ways different than I would like. I must still make the effort to do my best, not worrying about results, developing my ability to decide what I think is right and wrong while retaining the capacity to seek the truth. But that's not all. I also need to somehow grow in the reality of life's important mysteries by making decisions about what I believe, and then let what I experience reinforce or force me to reject these beliefs. Which brings me back to being willing to make the effort. In a world that often refuses to cooperate.

Now, just how am I supposed to do all that?

The answer is grace. Grace helps the willing accomplish all they need to accomplish on their faith journey.

"Grace is...the *free and undeserved help* that God gives us to respond to his call to become children of God, partakers of the divine nature and eternal life."[119] Grace is a form of love, a free gift, with no strings attached, which allows us to find God and the joy that is our destiny.

We receive grace through the action of the Holy Spirit.[120] As with all forms of love, grace requires our free response to be effective.[121] We must be willing to practice to become grace-full.

Grace can only be known and never fully understood, for grace is a mystery.[122] There are over one hundred references to it in the Catechism, none of which provide a full explanation. Almost every author I have read, and every speaker I have listened to, has had a slightly different approach to explaining it. The good news is that all agree it is real and available to those who seek it. It makes the journey possible. Even when we don't recognize it for what it is. The important point is a simple one: God is intimately involved in our journey whenever we are willing to let him be.

As with all mysteries, grace can be known. Just look for those unplanned and unexpected occurrences in your life that help you experience life and the reality of a loving God more completely. Even though you have little or nothing to do with their appearance on your life. My own journey has been filled with them: the love of a wonderful wife, a priest offering to play basketball with parishioners,

---

119 Catechism, 1996
120 Catechism, 2003
121 Catechism, 2002
122 Catechism, 2005

a marvelous Parish in Connecticut, my surprising willingness to go on a Cursillo retreat when asked by a near stranger, my daughter Michele asking for my help in running an Emmaus retreat, the incredible power I have witnessed in the rooms of Alcoholics Anonymous, my desire to become a Deacon, to name just a few. It's the reason I feel like I'm the luckiest person in the world. Grace is powerful stuff.

If you are willing to believe, take a few minutes and reflect on such occurrences in your own life. You may be surprised by your ability to see the power of grace at work.

Having said there is no complete explanation of grace, there is one metaphor that I find very helpful. It comes from Father Tony Mullane, the pastor I had the privilege of working with in the Florida Keys for fourteen years. He describes grace as energy, divine energy.

Energy allows us to act, think, and become more. Without energy, we are nothing, can do nothing. Divine energy helps us make the effort, develop our consciences, discern the truth, and make choices—the right choices. So we can grow in the knowledge of God and the other great mysteries.

Divine energy is also present in the power of love to heal and transform. Two Gospel stories might help illustrate this point.

When a woman who has suffered hemorrhages for twelve years touches the fringes of Jesus' clothing, she is healed. Jesus immediately senses what has happened because he feels energy leave him. He calls the woman to him and says to her, "Daughter, your faith has made you well; go in peace."[123] The woman experiences healing because she is open to the energy that emanates from Jesus. The same connection between healing and openness to Jesus' power is present in many of the healing miracles.

Another wonderful story about the nature of grace involves the parable of the prodigal son.[124] It is the story of two sons, one who makes all kinds of poor choices but ends up celebrating, another son who seems to make no wrong choices but doesn't, and a loving father who deals with them both in the same way. If you haven't read it recently, take a minute to do so before proceeding (Luke 15:11–32).

Most people see this story as a description of God's unconditional love and forgiveness. The father lets his younger son leave and make almost every conceivable mistake. When the younger son then comes to his senses and returns to admit his errors, the father refuses to

123   LK 8:48
124   LK: 15: 11-32

listen to the specifics of his confession and prepares a great feast for him. The younger son ends up better than he had ever imagined possible. God's forgiveness is a marvelous form of grace.

For me, however, the more impressive example of grace involves the son's decision to return. For it is the father's great love which allows the younger son to believe he will be allowed to rejoin his father's household. God's grace is more than just forgiveness, important as forgiveness is. Grace is God's way of giving us the strength to return to where we should be. It helps us "come to our senses" when we are willing to use it.

As the story ends, the older son, who on the surface of things has done everything right, remains on the outs, literally. Despite his father's pleading with him, reminding him, "All that is mine is yours," he refuses to join the celebration. The older son is unwilling to accept his father's goodness. He is unwilling to accept grace. He remains captive to his false pride and self-righteousness. Sometimes I wonder how often we practicing "Christians" are the older brother.

So what's the rule? Grace, God's way of using the Holy Spirit to help us live life to the fullest, is real. It is a free gift. As with any gift, it does us no good unless we take advantage of it. When we do, it makes the whole journey possible.

On Being Human

While each of us is unique, we all share many traits. One is our desire to be complete or perfect. Another is the fact none of us are yet. While God created each of us in goodness, he also created us incomplete.

Being human means we make mistakes. With the exception of Jesus and Mary, we have all been tempted and we have all sinned. Every one of us. When we expect perfection, of others or ourselves, we will always be disappointed. I can still remember the first time I realized my father was not perfect. It was a disorienting experience.

Since then, I have learned that much of what we love in another human being has its source in his or her imperfections. The crooked smile, hair that won't behave, my wife's inability to refrain from straightening whatever I'm wearing, my inability to keep whatever I'm wearing straight. Our shortcomings not only endear us to others, they highlight our good and unique qualities.

A long time ago, my wife and I encountered a woman about our age who was as close to perfect as anyone I have ever met. She looked and acted like Julie Andrews in *The Sound of Music*. She seemed to be in perfect control, with perfect manners, a perfect smile, and perfect children (for some reason I can't even remember her husband). When we were with her, it was like being in the presence of a perfectly crafted painting with no soul. My only emotion was detached admiration. Nothing else. There was nothing to identify with or relate to. In fact, she seemed so unreal she became boring.

Being human is the process of living and loving in imperfection while we grow and become more.

When the permanent diaconate program accepted me, my first task was to find a spiritual director. For those unfamiliar with spiritual directors, think of them as mentors on the spiritual journey. I asked a good friend of ours, Father Tom, whom we had come to know through our daughters. His first reaction was a definite "No," but after some thought he came back and said he would reconsider if I were willing to accept one reality. Fearing a demand to follow the rules of the Church more closely, I hesitated but eventually agreed.

Here is the reality I was asked to accept: the greatest proof of God's existence is that the Catholic Church has survived.

I was surprised and relieved. At the time, I could not have possibly guessed how often I would think of and reflect on the precious gift he had given me. For, as I was entering a new phase of my own journey, he was gently telling me that the Church may be perfect in the sense it is Divine in origin and is guided by the Holy Spirit, but the Church is run by humans. And all humans make mistakes. He was telling me I was setting myself up for disappointment or worse if I expected otherwise. Interestingly, as I have grown in my knowledge of just how human the Church is, my love for the Church has also grown.

It surprises many Catholics to know the Church acknowledges the humanity of its history.[125] It realizes all its members are imperfect, on a journey that requires patience and work and trust in God's goodness, with perfection something that will only be achieved at the end of time.[126] And that those ordained to the priesthood or diaconate, no matter how well intended, are subject to the same human frailties as the rest of us.[127]

Being human is the process of living and loving in imperfection while we strive to become more.

Some non-practicing, or sort-of-practicing, Catholics tell me they do not need religion. I just smile. Most, however, have one or more stories about mistakes made by the Church that led to their apathy. Interestingly, I can say the same for non-practicing or sort-of-practicing Christians of any denomination. The stories I hear tend to fall into one of three categories:

1. Past experiences that led to a feeling of rejection
2. Current experiences in the local Parish
3. The way the Church is being managed

Here's a sampling.

When I was growing up, all the priests and nuns talked about was what I couldn't do: sin and punishment and the dangers of sex and a whole bunch of rules. I could only do what I was told. Obey and believe, or get punished, by the nuns if no one else. No one ever mentioned love. I just couldn't relate.

My priest doesn't understand me. He always seems to follow the party line. He has no compassion. He is too absolute, too judgmental. His Masses are boring, his homilies are too long, he always seems to be talking about money. He's too busy to deal with my problems. He doesn't understand what's important. He doesn't care.

---

125 Catechism, 817
126 Catechism, 825
127 Catechism, 827

The Church is too slow to change. The Church's teachings are impossible for the normal person to understand. The Church is too black and white in a world filled with shades of gray. It treats too many things as absolutes. The Church doesn't understand sex. The language of the Church is too formulaic and exclusive. The Church discriminates against women. The sex abuse scandal is a disgrace. The Pope makes mistakes. The Vatican is out of touch. Too many members of the clergy think they are the center of the universe. Too many bishops worry too much about their own advancement. The Church doesn't understand me. The Church doesn't care. I'm just supposed to obey and believe what I'm told. I just can't relate.

I'm sure I missed some, but I think you get the idea.

While it's just my opinion, I plead guilty on all counts. Not always, not even most of the time, but I am sure everything I have mentioned, at some time in some place, has happened. I am also sure some have happened more often than others.

The common denominator of all these experiences is disappointment resulting from failed expectations. Those running our Church never were and still aren't perfect, sometimes not even close. And when one brick crumbles, the whole wall tumbles down. The more emotional and angry one is in describing his or her experience, the bigger the disappointment and resulting sense of abandonment. My point here is not to ignore or condone inappropriate behavior. My point is that we tend to have an unrealistic expectation level in our relationship with the Church. It is an expectation level that would not allow any relationship to survive.

I worked for International Business Machines for thirty years. IBM was a great company to work for and I was proud to be associated with it. In particular, IBM was known for the excellence of its management. But that management, of which I was a part, was human.

No matter what level of the company I was part of, it seemed to me those above me didn't understand my problems. Once I started rising in management, I was surprised how easy the jobs below me became. In a way it was like playing football. Football is a difficult, stressful, and often painful game on the playing field. I remember that from my high school days. Yet, the farther I got from the field the easier the game became.

The most difficult management job in any organization is the lowest or first level. Like being a priest in the Catholic Church. It is the only level of management that must deal with the ever-changing dynamics of the parishioner's world. Neither higher levels of management nor the parishioners being served understand the complexity of this balancing act, even though both assume they do. The only certainty is it is almost impossible to please both audiences at the same time.

It's hard to manage anything well, and the complexity increases with responsibility. It takes time, effort, and an endless balancing between long-term goals and short-term tactics in the midst of ever-changing challenges. As a result, there are several tempting shortcuts as one rises in management.

It is easier to talk with other members of management than with those on the "playing field." Over time, you even develop your own jargon in the name of more precise and complete communications, which only compounds the difficulty in communicating with anyone else. The higher you rise in an organization, the more people below you tell you what you want to hear rather than what you need to hear. There is an increasing temptation to become more absolute in your decisions in an effort to eliminate needless debate and to help those beneath you conform to company policies. This tendency becomes more pronounced in times of crisis.

It's surprisingly easy to become embroiled in internal debates. So much so you tend to forget the whole purpose of a corporation is to provide value to its customers. Think of it as forgetting who is the servant and who is the one served. There is an unspoken tendency to turn a blind eye to the truth to avoid embarrassment, evade responsibility for failure, or protect the company image. Finally, it is always easier to do nothing than to change.

Now, start with all these human tendencies, from a company known for the excellence of its management because it provided ongoing training to all levels of management. Transfer these tendencies to the human beings managing our Church who receive almost no training in any aspect of management. Then add the belief that God is not only on your side but has personally given you a mandate to straighten out the world. I think you can sense the potential for mischief. Particularly since the Holy Spirit, at least from the vantage point of history, seems to avoid hands-on management. Most of the time, the Holy Spirit appears to be much like the father in the prodigal son parable.

I know there are incompetent priests. However, the overwhelming majority of those I have met are hard working, dedicated human beings struggling to do their best, with little if any pay and almost no management support. The amazing thing to me is how many actually enjoy it. As I mentioned at the beginning of this book, I live in awe of these men.

As a permanent deacon in various Parishes, I had the opportunity to meet and interact with a fairly large number of these men. Gradually I formed a whole new way of deciding how I viewed them. Gone were my early childhood notions of perfection, and my tendencies as a young adult to condemn the smallest failings in their homilies, their inability to manage people or money the way I would like, or their tendency to micromanage. Gradually I decided there were only three criteria for deciding which priests I wanted to be my friends.

First, I look for a vibrant faith. I do not mean showy or necessarily charismatic. I mean a faith grounded in a deep belief that the Divine is present in each one of us. Second, I value a deep respect for our Traditions, reverence for our Mass, the Sacraments, and Church teachings, combined with the certainty they as individuals are the primary way most people will decide whether God is in fact a loving God. Finally, and in some ways most importantly, I look for a willingness to care. This was the first distinguishing characteristic of Jesus' healing miracles, and I know it is extremely difficult to do in the face of thoughtless criticism, careless judgment, and the threat of rejection. Yet, it is the priests who continue to care, the ones who refuse to withdraw from the battleground of life, that touch me most deeply. For they are the ones who work miracles.

I don't know many bishops. I am sure there are some whose primary interest is running the race to nowhere. I can understand that, for I have been there. However, the few I have had the privilege to interact with have been inspirational in their dedication, faith, and empathy for others. I marvel at the complexity and demands of their jobs.

Finally, I obviously have never met the Pope. I have been to the Vatican only once, as an ordinary tourist, and have little desire to return. So I can't comment on either based on personal experience. But here is what I do know. The Catechism calls all Catholic Christians to "obey" the Church. "Obey" is defined as being willing to "Listen to or hear in faith."[128] I think this is reasonable because it means we are responsible for understanding with an open mind and an open heart. I do not agree with everything the Vatican says. But I am willing to listen and hear because I have found that almost everything important said by the Vatican is based on principles I

128   Catechism, 144

84

agree with. I then follow my conscience. I think those who criticize a specific teaching of the Church or a specific statement from the Pope or the Vatican would do well to do the same.

My intent is not to argue the human management of our Church is perfect. My intent is to suggest nothing except God is. And the Church in its current form is not God. When we expect perfection from the Church or anyone else—yes, anyone—not only will we be disappointed, but we will miss the beauty of what is there.

In the case of the Catholic Church, what is there is precious beyond description. For over two thousand years one organization has not only survived but has managed to preserve a breathtaking set of beliefs, teachings, and resources whose only purpose is help imperfect humans on their journey to perfection; a free gift for anyone who wants to learn how to experience the joy of living life fully. From a God whose patience with us, like his love for us, is beyond description.

Obviously, many have split off from the Catholic Church in an effort to form a more perfect Church. Yet, it seems to me every version of Christianity, over time, develops its own set of imperfections. And the almost geometric increase in denominations in the last decade seems to indicate the treasure hunt for the perfect church will remain just that. In the meantime, I would like to suggest an alternative. Maybe God accepts that humans, with all their frailties, are the best he's going to get. Maybe, just maybe, he planned it that way. As part of the journey.

If God is willing to put up with us, why can't we do the same? Rather than focusing on what others aren't doing or ought to be doing, maybe we should spend more time thinking about what we aren't doing or ought to be doing. Because, in the end, that's what we have the power to change. And as we change, as we become more, so will our Church.

The way I look at it, as soon as I'm perfect, I'm going to start working on everyone else. Until then, I think I'll just try to make the effort and leave the results to God.

It seems to be a much simpler way of being human.

Becoming Who We Are

Trying to figure out why people are the way they are used to bother me. No matter how hard I tried, there didn't seem to be a simple explanation. Maybe it was my upbringing. When faced with some particularly dumb thing I had done, my mother would look at me pensively and then say, almost to herself, "I wonder—is it heredity or the way I brought you up?"

I now know that both are important. Our childhood experiences are particularly important when it comes to feeling loved and being able to develop trust. Our health, relationships, approach to spirituality, and many other factors also play a role in determining why we are the way we are. Sonja Lyubomirsky, author of the book I quoted earlier on happiness *(The How of Happiness: A Scientific Approach to Happiness)*, asserts that 50% of our "inherent" happiness level is determined by genetic factors, 10% by life's circumstances (the environment we live in), and the remaining 40% by 'intentional activity' (how we chose to live life)[129]. My point here is not to debate the specific numbers. Rather, it is to demonstrate what we all know intuitively: many things influence our happiness, as well as what might not be so obvious—the internal choices we make are much more important than the external trappings of life. Said another way, the fact "life happens" is not nearly as important as how we chose to deal with what we receive (four times more important if Ms. Lyubomirsky is correct).

Becoming who we are is a way of looking at the choices we make. The phrase is not mine but came from a friend who was listening to my confusion over two loved ones. They were in almost identical situations. One was positive, a joy to be with, and at peace. The other was argumentative, stubborn, and continually focusing on the problems in her life. I think I was still in the "I can fix anyone if I just try hard enough" phase of my life and so was confused.

His analysis was simple: people become who they are, meaning the attitudes they chose, whatever they are, will become increasingly pronounced as they age. Since then, I have heard the same thought expressed as "we become what we chose to do." Either way, I think the idea is the same because our attitudes play such a large role in determining what we do.

At the time, my friend's analysis gave me an explanation for my two loved ones. Since then, it has helped me understand one of the

129   *The How of Happiness*, Sonja Lyubomirsky, p. 20

major reasons people behave the way they do. It is included as one of the Rules of the Road because it is inherent in our makeup and because it is a gift God gives each of us: the ability to control what we become. A few brief examples might help demonstrate this point.

A young woman was faced with the reality of an unfaithful husband who refused to have children (which she longed for), drank too much, moved her to an area where she had no friends, and then within a year abandoned her. She had no way to support herself. Today she is still single and will never have her own children. However, she is a warm, loving, and serene person recognized for the artistic skills she has developed. She has a whole community who thinks of her as family and an array of kids she considers her children at the school where she works. When she tells her story, what strikes me is her courage to seek and accept help, her willingness to try new approaches, her determination to be an active part of her community, her focus on what might be rather than what was not. If you heard her story, you might be struck by different things, but I would be surprised if you didn't share my feeling of being in the presence of someone special.

An older man lived for years with his demons. As a child he had been punished severely by his father for any perceived wrongdoing. He developed a quick temper himself and slowly shut down his efforts to share with others, a process that was accelerated by frequent family moves. Bad habits like stealing started to become more commonplace. A stint in the Navy was followed by a failed attempt at one college and a barely successful time at another, despite counseling and almost constant probation. He had some successes that indicated a high level of intelligence, but an anger problem and an inability to form lasting relationships seemed to always get in the way. A marriage produced three children but ended in failure after nine years. Guilt over the failed marriage and shame for not properly caring for these children became his most intimate companions.

Today this same gentleman lives life with a smile on his face and a song in his heart. He goes out of his way to help others. The love of his second wife and their two children helped him to begin changing the way he viewed life and those around him. He found himself succeeding in a variety of fields. His decision to become actively involved in a small church community gave him a whole new perspective on the value of his relationships with the people God had placed in his life. I particularly loved watching him help an older widow filled with anger over what she perceived to be the problems of her life. He has reestablished contact with his first three children and has worked at being present to them. He has even come to understand that his demons will slowly vanish to the extent he is willing to forgive everyone in need of forgiveness, especially himself. If you met him, you would think, "Now, there's the kind of person I would like to be." You would never guess he has overcome so much. The last time I saw him, he and his wife were preparing to leave on an extended motorcycle trip. He had an impish grin on his face.

Finally, I would like to tell you about my younger brother Stephen and my good friend Jeanne. I use their names because I consider both part of my family. Steve and Jeanne have suffered from debilitating mental diseases their entire adult lives. Both have had complicating physical problems. They have suffered rejection and a feeling of helplessness. At times, they have been difficult to be with because life has been so difficult for them. Steve has been fortunate in having a loving wife to support him. Jeanne's husband left her when their children were young. In many ways, she makes me think of Job.

What amazes me about Steve and Jeanne is that they have lived life as fully as they have. They have experienced times of great joy. They know their children love them with an intensity that is hard to describe. They had the satisfaction of watching these children grow into loving spouses and parents. Steve and Jeanne chose to live their lives with a certainty that God is real and loves them, and that if they do their best, their best will be good enough. In my opinion, they succeeded in a way many of us would not have the strength or courage to emulate. In a very special way, they are my role models.

Recently Jeanne passed away. Her funeral Mass was filled with people who had both funny and deeply touching memories. There was a feeling that a very special person had left our midst. Her two children miss her terribly. It does little good when I remind them that, like Job, Jeanne is now enjoying abundance beyond her wildest dreams.

These are brief stories. I have met countless other people who have chosen to change their attitudes toward life, sometimes without even knowing that they are the ones making the choices! My experiences in AA could fill a book. God has personally have blessed me by placing people in my life to help me make good choices. In every case, a willingness to establish new attitudes has led to a deeper appreciation of the goodness in life.

Obviously, I have also encountered those who choose to live life waiting for the world to think as they do, or who feel they can do nothing about the way life is treating them, or who have concluded their situation is hopeless. The common denominator is an unwillingness to change, which seems to lead to a grayness of spirit and an inability to grow. I do not say this as judgment, but as a matter of observation. I pray for such people.

For those willing to risk changing themselves, the journey may be short or long, but it will always lead to a better place. Specific attitudes suggested by the Roman Catholic faith will be discussed later in this book, in the section on "Attitudes" in Chapter VI. For now, please accept that every choice you make has consequences, and the most important consequence is that choice's effect on you becoming who you are.

Summary

Ready vs. Willing

God calls those who are willing to make the journey. Being ready is not a requirement. Commitment is.

Life Happens

There will be times of triumph and times of failure, joy, disappointment, well-being, and suffering in our journey. Sometimes when we expect them, often when we don't. To conclude religion is a form of medication meant to anesthetize us to the trials of life misses the whole point of what Jesus was trying to accomplish.

God never promised an absence of storms, assurance of success, or even good health. He did not promise to change life. He did promise to help us change to become more complete. So we would know serenity in our difficulties, gratitude for our successes, and the reality of eternal life.

He also promised to bring good from whatever happens to us, if we are willing to trust in his love. To trust even when understanding fails. To be willing to live life rather than be buried by it, taking up our crosses, whatever they may be, and following him.

Effort vs. Results

Accepting that life has its ups and downs does not mean we must passively accept what comes our way. We are still responsible for making the effort. This includes discerning what's important, making choices, planning for the future, setting goals, doing our best. However, one of the hardest rules to implement is to avoid the expectation of specific results. We are responsible for the effort, not the results. Think of it as rowing the boat and leaving the steering to God.

Moral Conscience

Humans have embedded within them a capability to discern right from wrong, along with a natural inclination to do right. We call this capability moral conscience. Every human being is responsible for developing the gift of conscience. We call this formation of conscience, and it is a critically important responsibility. With a properly formed conscience, "Man has the right to act in conscience and in freedom to make moral decisions. He must not be forced to act contrary to his conscience. Nor must he be prevented from acting according to his conscience, especially in religious matters."[130] "In all he says and does, man is obliged to follow faithfully what he knows to be just and right."[131]

Sometimes it is difficult to know the right course of action. The Church suggests three rules that apply in all cases:

1. One may never do evil so that good may result from it. The end does not justify the means.
2. Remember the Golden Rule: Do onto others as you would have them do to you.
3. Respect others and their right to follow their conscience. Do nothing that harms either.[132]

Seeking Truth

Seek the truth. The Divine is present in the truth. An unwillingness to seek truth in favor of unquestioning adherence to currently held beliefs diminishes the grandeur of God and stifles growth. Growth requires change, and Jesus clearly calls us all to a lifelong willingness to change.

Mysteries

When applied to things spiritual, a mystery is a truth or reality that can be known but never fully understood.

Believe and You Will See

Like Thomas, most of us believe something once we have seen the evidence to prove its existence. Jesus taught that spiritual sight does not precede but follows a decision to believe.

Grace

Grace helps the willing accomplish all they need to accomplish on their faith journey. We receive grace through the action of the Holy Spirit. Think of grace as divine energy.

On being human

All humans are incomplete. We have all been tempted and have all sinned. While the Church is holy in the sense it is inspired and guided by the Divine, humans run the Church. The Catholic Church acknowledges the imperfections of its members, including the

130   Catechism, 1782
131   Catechism, 1778
132   Catechism, 1787

ordained,[133] as well as the fact we will reach perfection only at the end of time.[134]

When we expect perfection from members of the Church or anyone else, not only will we be disappointed, but we will miss the beauty of what is there. In the case of the Church, what is there is precious beyond description.

Becoming who we are

Attitudes toward life and others will become more pronounced the longer we hold them. We will become more of who we are. We control who we will be in the future.

133   Catechism, 817, 827
134   Catechism, 769

V
Gifts

In Brief

Have you ever noticed how easy it is to take for granted what is most precious to us? Like water, the food we eat, music, those we love, colors, even the air we breathe. I guess it's part of the human condition.

The whole point of the next two chapters is this: God has given each of us certain capabilities and capacities, which, although we largely take them for granted, can help us on the journey. This chapter is called "Gifts" because I want to call attention to the fact we did nothing to earn or deserve what is covered. In addition, they are ours without condition. All we need to do is recognize their value.

Of course, the subjects covered in the next chapter are also gifts, but they require more active participation on our part to realize the full benefit of what God has given us. Hence, I have chosen to call them choices.

Neither chapter is meant to be all-inclusive. In fact, I hope they prompt you to think of other things that have helped you in your life. That, after all, is the primary point of the chapters. Because you then will be experiencing one of God's great gifts: gratitude. It is impossible to be discouraged or disappointed or unhappy when you are experiencing gratitude. In fact, when I feel grateful for one part of my life, it often causes me to think of other things for which I am also grateful. I call these moments "gratitude attacks." I just wish I would remember to experience them more often!

One request. I have listed a Scripture reference at the beginning of each section in both "Gifts" and "Choices." Please take a moment and read the passage(s) before you start reading. Use any Bible you are comfortable with. If you don't have one, or would like to make sure you are using a "Catholic" Bible, I would recommend three: the New Jerusalem Bible; the NRSV (New Revised Standard Edition) Bible, Catholic Edition; and the New American Bible for Catholics. Scripture passages used in the Mass come from the New American Bible for Catholics. I use the NRSV because I believe it may be a more accurate translation. My sentimental favorite is the New Jerusalem Bible because it was the first Bible I ever tried to read seriously. My wife Frannie gave it to me as I was starting my Diaconate training. I was deeply touched by the gift, and to this day I am still grateful for it.

Home

Matthew 4:1–11

Some time ago, my wife and I were in Chicago visiting one of our daughters. While we were there it occurred to me I was only a forty-minute drive from the home I had lived in as a youngster. My son-in-law graciously agreed to join me for the trip, and the next day we set off with high expectations.

As we approached the old neighborhood I was filled with excitement. Family memories from early childhood came to me so clearly I felt I was reliving them. I was completely unprepared for what I found.

The steep hills I used to struggle up and race down on my first bike were much smaller than I remembered, some being little more than small rises and dips in the road. Large trees, mature hedges, and far too many houses had taken the place of what was once almost completely open terrain with a smattering of new plantings surrounding relatively few homes. With a start, I realized I had conveniently forgotten it had been almost fifty years since my last visit.

As a result, I was completely unprepared when we came around the bend in the road to discover that the home I had lived in had been torn down. In its place stood what seemed to me to be a large stone monstrosity. As we slowed the car, my eyes filled with tears. The place where I had first learned I was loved just as I was, where I had learned to forgive because I had been forgiven, where I learned mistakes are really just lessons learned, where everything seemed to belong[135]...this place was gone.

On the trip back to Chicago, I reflected on my experience. I realized we all have a deep yearning for home. But this home has little to do with a geographic place. Home is wherever we know we are loved as we are, forgiven so we can forgive, and accepted so completely that mistakes fade to mere lessons learned, allowing us to live with a sense that everything belongs. I believe God has created us with this yearning. This is a free gift.

We satisfy this yearning when we become part of a family where members know they don't have to be perfect; they just have to share the depth of their love, the fact that they care. Where they know they are accepted just as they are. And they know other members feel as responsible for their welfare as they do. We all value the gift

---

135   Richard Rohr

of family. What surprises most of us is how much freedom we have in choosing our families.

Each one of us starts with some form of traditional family. For most this a positive experience, even though all families have disagreements and shortcomings. I think accepting this reality—that no family is perfect—greatly increases our capacity for taking advantage of the benefits of family. At the same time, there are some whose traditional family experience has no redeeming qualities, which makes it even more important to realize that traditional family is just the first of many families we can join.

Obviously, as we mature most of us find a spouse to share our lives with. Whether we have children or not, we have become part of a new family. But that is just the beginning. Almost without recognizing it, we become part of a group of close friends, in a neighborhood, a work department, some club, or Parish community, to name a few examples. Whenever we become part of a group where we are willing to care, knowing others in the group will return our affection with caring of their own, we have become part of another family. Our range of choices is truly amazing. What we often miss is that these choices are critically important to our well-being, because they help determine how soon or even if we will find home.

During the early 1990s, I discovered and fell in love with salt-water fly-fishing. Since traveling to the Bahamas to satisfy my craving was quite expensive, my wife started encouraging me to try the Florida Keys. And so we did. I soon discovered the Keys were an excellent place to pursue what became a decade long passion of fly-fishing for an elusive fish called the permit.

Our second or third visit to the Keys included a weekend, so we decided to attend Mass at the local church, St. Peter's on Big Pine Key. As we approached the front door, a woman stepped forward and, holding out her hand, and said something like, "Welcome, it is SO good to have you here with us today." As we walked inside we immediately sensed we were part of a very special community. People were smiling, making an effort to introduce themselves, asking us if we would like to attend an upcoming Parish event.

Thus began a fourteen-year love affair that transformed both of us in ways difficult to even put into words. What is clear is we profited immeasurably from the experience.

The pastor, Father Tony, one of the most accepting yet self-assured people we had ever met, became a close friend. We worked, we played, we laughed, and we prayed together. There were moments of great fun, times of challenging difficulties, and an ever-increasing circle of close friends we could not imagine living without. We became part of a very special family that allowed us to taste the joy of coming home, creating memories we will treasure forever.

While at St. Peter's I was asked to teach a Bible study course at a local prison. It was a minimum-security facility where the inmates tended to be there for multiple years, so I had the opportunity to get to know them quite well. What surprised me was how consistently these men, whom I found to be humorous, generous, and warm-hearted individuals, had made poor choices in the families they had chosen to join: sex-based relationships without responsibility; drinking or drug-addicted friends; small groups specializing in housebreaking, shoplifting, and other forms of petty crime; and territorial gangs. These were broken families, and as a result they were now broken men, wondering what to do next.

Several years ago, we decided it was time to relocate to a life care community (meaning independent living, with assisted living and full time nursing care available if and when needed) in Juno Beach, FL. We made the decision to do so at a relatively young age because one must be healthy to be accepted and, as cancer survivors, we are both faced with the possibility of a reoccurrence at any time.

The Waterford has proven to be a wonderful place to live. As sorry as we were to leave St. Peter's, we have never regretted our decision.

One of the main reasons for this feeling is the new Parish community we found in North Palm Beach, Florida. The first time we went to Mass, I was still using crutches from recent foot surgery. My wife dropped me off and went to park the car. As I hobbled up to the front door, feeling sorry for myself and missing our friends at St. Peter's who would have helped me into the church, the door magically opened, and a smiling man I had never seen before said, "Welcome; here, let me help you." He carefully led me to a pew where I could sit without unduly disturbing others, leaving me with the comment, "Let me know if there is anything else I can do."

I knew someone cared. I felt accepted. And that was our first visit to a Parish that has since become a major source of spiritual and emotional nourishment for both Frannie and me.

This is just one of three Parishes we currently consider family. The other two are in central New Hampshire. We have been part of these communities so long we have seen our small satellite mission church absorbed into two Parishes presided over by one pastor. That pastor is our friend Father Edmund.

I first met Father Edmund when he was pastor for a Parish well to our south. He seemed very happy being an integral part of a small community, knowing and interacting with almost everyone. One of his favorite pastimes was watching *The Sopranos* each week with pastors or rectors from the other religious denominations in town.

One day, quite unexpectedly, his comfortable world disappeared. The Bishop gave him an additional Parish to oversee. At that moment, he knew he would never again be the intimately involved pastor in one small community.

Over the next six months I watched Fr. Edmund struggle with this reality. At one point I feared he would just give up and retreat into a shell of indifference. Then, almost miraculously, a new Father Edmund slowly emerged. His faith was more alive, not in a showy fashion but in a way I envied. His sense of humor returned as he became more active, but active with a new sense of just doing the best he could with the time and talent he had. I think he had decided to trust more completely in the goodness of God. Today, he is a joy to encounter. Both Parishes are larger than before they were twinned, even though both Parishes were forced to close mission churches. I have learned a great deal from my friend's experience.

The families we choose to be part of are so important to satisfying our yearning for home because they are where we acquire our life principles. A life principle is a subconscious guide that shapes how we view life and make everyday decisions. We develop these principles, usually a small number, as part of learning how to deal with the ever-changing nature of life. In almost all cases, they grow out of our efforts to emulate the behavior of role models in our families. Father Edmund is one of my role models.

Naturally, our family of origin is crucially important in this process. My prison Bible study students came overwhelmingly from highly dysfunctional family environments. I feel very fortunate to have come from a loving family of origin. At the same time, the families we form or become part of as we mature can play a surprisingly significant role in helping us change old life principles or form new ones. The Parish communities my wife and I participate in continue to mold the way we view and deal with life.

Matthew's well-known account of Jesus' temptations summarizes three of the most common life principles. We call them temptations because they are perceived shortcuts to happiness, to coming home, when in fact they are all paths to nowhere, each one creating a never-ending thirst for more of the same.

The first we can call the Provider. I provide. Others will love me, others will forgive me my shortcomings, and everything will belong, when I provide enough.

This temptation, like all temptations, seems rational at first blush. After all, Jesus was hungry when the tempter approached him and suggested he turn stones into bread. Aren't we supposed to provide what others need or what we need for ourselves? The problem is no one can live on bread alone, and a preoccupation with providing leads to a preoccupation with providing more, with the resulting overemphasis on the material aspects of life. Small wonder that anxiety and stress, as well as rates of substance abuse, suicide, and divorce, are so high among the more affluent.

The second temptation can be called the Performer. I perform so you will know I am important. Others will love me, respect me, and overlook my shortcomings when I prove I am important enough.

Original sin was not Adam and Eve eating an apple. It was not Adam and Eve breaking a rule. Original sin was Adam and Eve, and all of us ever since, wanting to be like God. To be important. To have others recognize our importance. To be the center of our universe.

Unfortunately, when I become the center of my universe, it is a lonely place to be. For it is a universe of one.

The third temptation can be called the Powerful. I will conquer all the kingdoms of the world. Other will love me, forgive my mistakes, everything will belong, when I am in charge.

Now very few of us say, "I am going to conquer kingdoms." No, most of us probably say something like "If I were in charge, things would be better," or "Things would be just fine if everyone just did as I asked them." But power, when given free reign, tends to starve the impulse to love, when love alone should be served.

As we all know, Jesus resisted the three temptations presented to him in the desert. What is not as apparent, until we think about it, are the life principles that did govern his life. I think this is because we seldom think of Jesus as someone we can model our lives after. To do so, however, takes but two small decisions. First, do not focus on Jesus the Christ (the divine Son of God), someone we worship as a member of a Trinitarian God, but Jesus of Nazareth, a human being like us in all things but sin. Secondly, do not try to emulate the specific activities Jesus chose to undertake. The vast majority of us do not have a vocation to leave everything to live in celibate poverty. Rather, try to discern and then imitate the way he chose to view life in every day situations. I think you may well be surprised by the result.

One of the advantages of reading and then meditating on the Gospels is the growing awareness of what was most important to Jesus. Throughout his life, Jesus consistently rejected the importance of wealth and material things as paths to happiness. He consistently avoided any attempt to make himself important or powerful. In their place, eagerness to do his Father's will, combined with humility, compassion and forgiveness were the hallmarks of the way Jesus chose to live his life. These were the life principles that governed his every decision.

We will talk more about these life principles in later chapters. For now, let's just summarize the idea behind them as the willingness to seek the goodness in others, to share without condition, and to trust always in the goodness of God and ourselves. In a word, love. Love as I have loved you.[136]

I doubt any of us can do these things perfectly. I know I can't, and I know I often fail. I also know:

Jesus knows I am not yet perfect.
Jesus does not ask me to achieve any specific result.
Jesus asks me only to make the effort.
Even when the effort is difficult,
When sacrifice is called for.
When loneliness, separation, even rejection, are the coin of this realm.
And be willing to pick myself up and try again.
When I fall, or fail, or forget.
Letting go of what is done, so I can begin anew.
One person, one laugh, one tear at a time.
Until my journey ends.
In his home.
Love without condition, love I have never fully tasted.
Forgiveness no longer needed, lessons all learned,
Because everything belongs.
Forever.

---

136   John: 15:12

Mary As Role Model

Luke 1:26–38; Luke 1:46–49
My soul magnifies the Lord.
My sprit rejoices in God, my savior,
For the Mighty One has done great things for me.
And holy is his name. [137]

Mary is an important figure in Roman Catholicism. We refer to her as Virgin Mary, Queen of Heaven, Mother of God, and Mother of the Church. When I say "Mother of God" and "Mother of the Church," I find myself adding "my Mother." Because Mary is one of my most important role models.

This was not always the case.

Growing up, I was bothered by what I perceived to be an excessive preoccupation with Mary in my parochial school classes. I am not sure why. Sometimes I think I was having a hard enough time assimilating the idea of Jesus as both God and man, although perhaps I was simply unable to sit still whenever the rosary was said. Eventually, I decided all the talk about Mary was caused by my religion's inability to recognize the feminine aspects of the Divine. So I stopped thinking about the subject.

But then, in the midst of dealing with my alcoholism, at the point when I finally knew something had to change, I found myself asking Mary to pray for me. Every morning. I just couldn't think of a better idea. Of course, when I finally started to get sober, I forgot about having prayed to her. Until several years later, when I was asked to speak on why Mary is so important to Roman Catholics.

For the first time, I realized I had to stop relying on my grade school prejudices. I decided to study Mary, understand what others had to say about her, meditate on her role in my life, and follow where she would lead me (assuming she would). In the process I developed my own view of why Mary is important. I recognize it might be at odds with what others think. But at least it is mine.

My first task was to understand why Mary is so prominent in Roman Catholic thinking. The answer is actually quite simple. We believe in ongoing revelation in the form of Tradition. Over the centuries, Mary has appeared in more apparitions or visions, or whatever you want to call them, than any other biblical figure. As a result we have been able to slowly develop an appreciation of Mary

---

137   LK 1: 46, 49

that both complements and expands on what Scripture has given us.

A personal experience helped me internalize this reality. While working in a south Florida Parish during the 1990s, I was invited to accompany a college professor asked by the Vatican to investigate alleged apparitions in that area. One of the individuals we visited, a pleasant middle-aged woman with no exposure to Roman Catholicism, claimed the Virgin Mary appeared to her periodically to request she convey a message to the world. She readily agreed to repeat what she had been told so we could understand what she thought Mary was saying.

When she started speaking, I was surprised by the woman's use of Roman Catholic terminology and teaching (e.g. Mother of God, full of grace, Mother of the Church, the rosary), even though she had had no exposure to our faith tradition. I was also struck by how formal the language was. The message itself centered on a call to seek, trust in, and pray for her Son's mercy at a time of increasing evil in the world. I was fascinated by what the woman had to say and how she said it. I thanked the college professor profusely for inviting me to join him. I then promptly forgot about the whole experience.

Until that summer when a parishioner in my New Hampshire Parish called and asked if I would participate in a Tuesday evening prayer group at our local church. Thinking this would be a great opportunity to explore different prayer forms in a relaxed setting, I readily agreed. Needless to say, I was more than a little surprised when I arrived to find we were going to say not one but three rosaries!

After the third rosary (my knees were killing me), the parishioner who had called me asked us all to sit (thank God). He then announced he was going to read passages from a diary of a South American priest who claimed Mary had visited him. We were told we would then discuss what he had read.

As he started reading I immediately realized the words were familiar. Yet, I had never heard of this South American priest. My momentary confusion slowly gave way to a stunning realization. It was as though time had stopped. The same terminology. The same formal language. I could feel the goose bumps. The passage I was listening to contained words almost identical to what I had heard the previous winter in Florida. I could think of only one rational explanation. Mary is not a figment of someone's imagination. Mary is real.

Mary is real. Mary cares. Mary is reaching out to us. She is calling us to seek her son's mercy. To help us find our way home.

Interestingly, this awakening happened years before I first learned about Jesus' call for us to seek, trust in, and pray for Divine Mercy.

Try and imagine your first reaction when you are told someone you hardly know cares for you. When you realize he or she thinks you are special and wants to be your friend. Don't you feel drawn to this person?

This was how I started to view Mary.

My earlier decision to pray for Mary's help in dealing with alcoholism came back to me. She had helped. Sure, I did my part. Many others had also been there for me. But my prayers had been answered. I realized I had never even thanked her for her assistance. So I did. And then I started praying to her more often. I'm not sure why, but I tend to ask for her help in matters affecting my daughters. An objective observer could probably give many reasons for our eldest daughter's recent return to the Church. But I know whom to thank.

There is understandable confusion about this business of praying to Mary. The idea is NOT to treat Mary as God, equal to God, or part of God. The idea is to ask for her help in praying to her Son. This makes sense to me. Because I know from past experience that the best way to get my attention was to have my mother on your side.

There is a human tendency to make people important to us into something other than who they really are. To focus only those aspects we feel most comfortable with, to the exclusion of all others. For example, there has been a tendency in Roman Catholicism to focus more on Jesus' divinity and less on his humanity. In the early formative stages of Christianity this tendency actually led to a heresy called Gnosticism. It is the reason we say we believe in Jesus Christ, the only Son of God, true God and true man.

There are many who still feel more comfortable with a Cosmic Christ, the name often given to the Divine Son of God, rather than wrestling with the ongoing mystery of Jesus of Nazareth as both true God and true man. I can understand why this happens, but I also believe a great deal is lost when we ignore how the human Jesus dealt with life.

I bring this up because I found a similar tendency in the books I read and the people I talked to about Mary. After a good deal of reflection, I made a decision. Even though I envy those who are fed spiritually through their identification with the more cosmic Virgin Mary, I find myself drawn to how she chose to live her life.

Surprisingly little is known about the historical Mary of Nazareth. Early Christian writings name her father as Joachim and her mother as Anne. The only generally agreed-to source we have about her life is the New Testament, specifically in passages contained in the Gospels of Matthew, Luke, and John. These accounts start when she was being betrothed to Joseph, most likely in her early teens. There are at least two theories concerning what happened to Mary after Jesus' death and Ascension. Some believe she lived in Ephesus with the disciple John. Others have her remaining in the Jerusalem area. The Catholic Church teaches her life on this earth ended when she was assumed, body and soul, into heaven (Feast of the Assumption), without taking a definitive position on whether or not she had died.

While the Gospel commentary of her life is relatively brief, there is much one can learn from reflecting on what it teaches us.

Mary most likely thought of herself as an ordinary teen before her encounter with the Angel Gabriel. While she may have been more religious than most, it is clear from her initial reaction to Gabriel that she was surprised ("she was much perplexed by his words and pondered what sort of greeting this might be"[138]). She probably knew no one expected anything significant to happen in Nazareth. She was also most probably focused on her coming marriage. Yet, one day an angel appeared to her, proclaiming she had found favor with God.

As I have already mentioned, God does many unexpected things in Scripture. Just one is reaching out to and depending upon what appear to be the most ordinary people. God can see something in them the individuals themselves cannot yet see. Sometimes I wonder how often we miss God's invitation to a deeper relationship because it comes in an unexpected way.

What most of those called by God have in common (e.g. Abraham, Moses, David, the prophets, Joseph, Mary and the apostles) is openness to God's invitation. They are disposed to say yes to God's will. They are willing. Yet, of all these people, I think Mary stands out as an extraordinary role model for how to deal with the Divine.

She is surprised but unafraid. She has the presence of mind to ask for clarification: "How can this be, since I am a virgin?"[139] In effect, she is asking, "Is this really God's will?" She listens to the

---

138 LK 1:29
139 LK 1: 34

104

explanation: "Nothing is impossible for God."[140] And then she says yes. She says yes by stating that her whole reason for being is to do the will of God: "Here I am, the servant of the Lord"[141] and by committing herself to that will: "Let it be done to me according to your word."[142]

In saying yes, Mary adds no qualifications. She does not say she in unworthy or undeserving. She never asks if, whether, or why[143]. She simply opens herself completely and without reservation to the God she trusts completely. Alone, quietly, and with courage.[144] In doing so, she exemplifies how to receive the grace of God. She does what you and I have such a hard time doing: accepting we do not have to deserve, earn, or be worthy; we merely must accept the great gift God offers us. "In God's eyes, our worthiness is given. It is not attained. It is God in us searching for God. It is God in us that believes and hopes and cares and loves. There is nothing we can take credit for. It is something we just thank God for." [145]

In saying this first yes, Mary was committing herself to many other yeses. She would have to deal with a skeptical fiancé in a society that killed unmarried pregnant women. She would then raise her child only to lose him, first to his public ministry and then to his death. She would have to suffer the pain of her son's rejection by the religion he cherished. She would then have to endure the humiliation of watching him die as the worst kind of criminal, for all intents and purposes deserted by his followers.

I wonder if ever, in the midst of some heartache or other disappointment, Mary remembered the angel's promises: "Your son...will be great, and will be called the son of the Most High, and the Lord God will give him the throne of his ancestor David. He will reign...forever and his Kingdom will have no end."[146] I wonder if she ever remembered these words and just slowly shook her head, a sad smile on her face.

While we don't know her thoughts, we do know she never failed to trust in her God. She was faithful to the end. In fact, perhaps the

---

140   LK 1: 37
141   LK 1:38
142   LK 1:38
143   Richard Rohr, 6/2/11 Richard's Daily Meditation
144   Richard Rohr, 6/2/11 Richard's Daily Meditation
145   Richard Rohr, 5/30/11 Richard's Daily Meditations
146   LK 1: 32-33

most famous statue of her, the one by Michelangelo of Mary holding her dead son, is called *PIETÀ*. The word means "faithfulness."[147]

Mary is one of my most important role models. I try to emulate her openness to the Divine, her humble trust in his will, and her perseverance. I also try to remember God did not do as the angel had promised. He did something better, something I doubt Mary ever imagined. Her son is now called the Son of the Most High, reigning over a Kingdom that will last forever, coequal with his Father. And Mary is now Queen of heaven, Mother of God, Mother of the Church, and, thank God, my mother.

My soul magnifies the Lord.
My sprit rejoices in God, my savior,
For the Mighty One has done great things for me.
And holy is his name.[148]

---

147 *Seasons of the Heart,* John Powell, S.J., p. 143
148 LK 1: 46, 49

Divine Mercy

Luke 15:1–7; John 20:19–31

The Gospels make clear that many of those who considered themselves good, especially the more religious, struggled with Jesus' idea of mercy. They were mystified by his willingness to associate with sinners, his refusal to let religious customs (like observance of the Sabbath) prevent him from helping those in need, and his assertion he could and would forgive sins. In addition, they found his teachings about mercy baffling. How could prostitutes and tax collectors enter the kingdom of heaven before religious leaders? How could the father forgive the prodigal son?

It seems not much has changed in the two thousand years since. For example, why would anyone ever leave ninety-nine sheep to find just one?[149] And then call his or her friends together to celebrate finding this one wayward sheep? Would you leave ninety-nine percent of everything important to you to find the lost one percent? I know I wouldn't. But Jesus claimed God does. Jesus' message: God will go to any length to save the sinner who has lost his way.

What makes this story so thought provoking is Jesus' statement "There will be more joy in heaven over one sinner who repents than over ninety nine righteous people who have no need of repentance."[150] When you think about it, who has no need of repentance (sincere regret for one's mistakes)? In one sentence, Jesus was doing two things. He was describing God's willingness to seek out each one of us in an effort to save us, because we all need repentance. At the same time he was calling into question the religious leaders' assumption they were so righteous they had no need of repentance.

How often are we those religious leaders?

By what he said and did, Jesus taught that his father's mercy was greater, richer, and more complete than any human concept of mercy. He confronted common religious beliefs of his day because they tended to depict God as the ultimate rule maker and religion as a simple matter of meeting one's obligations, or God as a scorekeeper who invented religion as a way to understand how to pass this test called life, or God as a judge who created religion as a way to dispense justice. Jesus asked his followers to realize they did not have to prove they deserved God's love; they just had to accept it. Accept God's

---

149   LK: 15: 1-7
150   LK 15: 7

mercy to help them overcome their inevitable missteps in trying to love as his Son had asked them to love.

As we all know, those who struggled with Jesus' teachings in first-century Israel rarely took time to listen to or reflect on what he said. Once again, I am afraid an impartial observer could say the same about us. All too often, we assume God's mercy is just something we hope to experience in the next life.

During the 1930s, a Polish nun, Sister Faustina Kowlaska (who became a Saint in 2000), wrote a six-hundred-page diary recording the revelations she received from Jesus concerning God's merciful love. For several decades the diary went largely unnoticed, until the late Pope John Paul II became personally involved based on his conviction the revelations were authentic.

The fundamental message contained in this diary is eerily similar to Jesus' teachings two thousand years earlier: God's mercy is infinite, is available to all, and comes from a God who longs for us to recognize and seek it.

The message of Divine Mercy is simple. It is that God loves us—all of us. And, he wants us to recognize that his mercy is greater than our sins, so that we will call upon him with trust, receive his mercy, and let it flow through us to others. Thus, all will come to share His joy.

The Divine Mercy message is one we can call to mind simply by remembering ABC:

A - Ask for His Mercy. God wants us to approach Him in prayer constantly, repenting of our sins and asking Him to pour His mercy out upon us and upon the whole world.
B - Be merciful. God wants us to receive His mercy and let it flow through us to others. He wants us to extend love and forgiveness to others just as He does to us.
C - Completely trust in Jesus. God wants us to know that the graces of His mercy are dependent upon our trust.

The more we trust in Jesus, the more we will receive.[151]

Sister (now Saint) Faustina's writings have led to a set of new devotional practices (most noticeably the Divine Mercy Chaplet), several new shrines, and the celebration of Divine Mercy Sunday once a year. When I take time to step back and think about it, however,

151 *The Divine Mercy Website*, Marions of the Immaculate Conception, home page

I am confused. I like the idea of sharing in joy. I like the idea of a mercy so complete and available to me that I need never obsess about my missteps. So why did Jesus have to come and remind us of what he had already told us in Sacred Scripture?

Why don't we care about Divine Mercy? What are we missing? What can we do about it?

Why don't we care?

The answer has to do with two of our Rules of the Road: "Mysteries" and "Believe and You Will See."

We are all like Thomas when he was first told about Jesus' appearance to his fellow disciples. We like to believe what we can see, what can be touched or experienced by one of the other senses. Or can be proved by logical reasoning, suspecting everything that can't be proven. It's the way we have been brought up, the way we have been taught to think.

The problem is the most important things in life can never be proven or fully understood; they can only be known. They are mysteries. And the five greatest mysteries are love, suffering, death, God, and eternity. [152]

Anyone who has experienced the immensity of great love knows there is no rational way to understand or explain it. We are reduced to using metaphors: I only have eyes for you, I am walking on air, my heart is bursting. Anyone who has experienced great suffering, such as the soul-searing grief associated with the sudden and unexpected loss of a loved one, knows there is no rational way to understand or explain it. And yet, it consumes a person for longer than most would like.

Great love and great suffering cannot be touched or seen. Neither can be fully understood; yet, we know both are very real. Death, God, and eternity are similar, with an added difficulty: No one we know personally has yet encountered death, God, or eternity and come back to describe it to us.

Imagine poor Thomas! His friends were asking him to deal with the mysteries of suffering, death, and a God who had just raised his son from the dead.

The primary reason most of us don't care about Divine Mercy is that Divine Mercy is a mystery, part of the mystery of great love. Mysteries can never be understood; they can only be experienced.

When we hear the word "mercy" it tends to conjure up images of an overly stern judge unexpectedly reducing the punishment

---

152 *The Naked Now*, Richard Rohr

of a clearly guilty wrongdoer. This is NOT what Jesus was talking about.

Most of us have never experienced anything close to the kind of mercy Jesus described and offered. Father James Keenan, a Jesuit theologian from Boston College, describes this mercy as the willingness to enter the chaos of another, on the other person's terms, your only objective being that person's well-being.[153] I can point to very few times in my life when I knew someone was TRULY with me, on MY terms, their ONLY objective being my well-being. One occurred when I was very young and very sick. My mother stayed up all night, just to be with me. I have never forgotten it. What I didn't realize at the time is I had experienced a glimpse of the reality called Divine Mercy.

Thomas had an advantage when Jesus came to him that we seldom discuss. It wasn't just that Jesus was present, as marvelous as that must have been. It was that Thomas was experiencing Divine Mercy first hand. Jesus came into the chaos of the life of those who had deserted him, their leader having denied him three times. They were alone in a room with their fear, behind locked doors both times. And he came to be with them, on their terms. When he spoke, he did not condemn, judge, or try to teach them. He simply said, "Peace be with you." During his first visit, he then gave those present the Holy Spirit, so they could forgive sins. When he came the second time, he invited Thomas to do what he needed to do so he could join his brothers in knowing the reality of the risen Lord. Jesus' only objective was the well-being of those he loved. No wonder Thomas said, "My Lord and my God."[154]

Jesus then said something very important for us. "Blessed are those who have not seen and yet have come to believe."[155] For those of us who have yet not experienced the mystery of God's mercy, or cannot yet recognize the times we have, it is important we be willing to believe, so we too can see.

When we are willing to consciously decide Divine Mercy is real and part of our lives, and then let our lived experience confirm (or force us to reconsider) our decision, we are doing what we have to do to realize all the greatest mysteries of life are authentic. This approach should not be foreign to us, for it is exactly what we do when we first learn to love another human being.

---

153   *St. Anthony Messenger Press,* April, 2010 Issue
154   JN 20:28
155   JN: 20:29

One of the stories Luke tells about God's mercy involves ten lepers who approach Jesus as he travels between Samaria and Galilee. In response to their plea, "Jesus, have mercy on us," Jesus tells them to go show themselves to the priests (priests held the power to determine that someone was no longer leprous and could therefore return home). As they go they are all cured. Only one, a Samaritan, realizes he has been healed and returns to Jesus to praise God for his great mercy. [156]

Those of you who have heard this story know the most prevalent interpretation focuses on the nine lepers who, even though they know they have been healed, do not return to Jesus to give thanks.

One of the things I love about Jesus' parables and healing miracles is that there are almost always multiple lessons available to those willing to look for them. In this case, I was struck one day by this thought: what if only one returned because only one was able to accept (see) he had been healed? The other nine continued to act as if they were diseased because they, like most of us, refused to believe in the power of God's mercy.

Most of us don't care about Divine Mercy because most of us can't see that the unimaginable gift of Divine Mercy is real. As a result, we cannot see the times we have experienced that mercy. Why was my mother with me all night when I was sick as a young child? I now KNOW the answer. God is love, and when I experience love in its purest form I experience the Divine. Divine Mercy.

What are we missing?

Scripture demonstrates that God has a passionate concern for our well-being. "As a mother comforts her child, so will I comfort you....You shall see, and your heart shall rejoice."[157] "Can a woman forget her nursing child, or show no compassion for the child of her womb? Even these may forget, yet I will not forget you. See, I have inscribed you on the palms of my hands." [158]

During his public ministry, Jesus was always ready to forgive when forgiveness was sought. When the criminal said, "Jesus, remember me when you come into your Kingdom," Jesus replied, "Truly I tell you, today you will be with me in Paradise."[159] Think about it. Jesus was breaking all the rules. Who forgives a convicted criminal based on one brief request? Who would ever promise everlasting joy to a

---

156   LK 17: 11-16
157   Isaiah 66:13-14
158   Isaiah, 49:15-16
159   LK 23:42-43

murderer? At a time when your own pain is overwhelming? And yet, that is exactly what Jesus did.

Jesus was always ready to heal whenever healing was sought. He never refused anyone who wanted to be healed. "Then Jesus said to him, 'What do you want me to do for you?' The blind man said, 'Teacher, let me see....' Jesus said to him, 'Go; your faith has made you well.' Immediately he regained his sight...."[160]

Can this passionate concern really apply to you and me?

For example, what about those who have experienced the pain and disorientation of divorce? Whenever someone mentions feeling unworthy because of a divorce, I tell that person the story of the woman at Jacob's well.

Jesus stops at a well while traveling through Samaria. His disciples go off to find some food. A woman approaches to get water, and Jesus engages her in conversation. She is surprised because a good Jew (and Jesus certainly was a good Jew) would NEVER address a Samaritan woman. Besides, this woman had had five husbands and is now living with a sixth man. Yet, Jesus senses she needs help. So he initiates the conversation.

The important point for us is not what they discussed but that Jesus did not stop interacting with the woman until she gained what she needed to live life more fully.[161] Do you think Jesus cared for this woman more than he cares for you and me?

Please, my brothers and my sisters, never lose sight of why the Divine entered human history in the form of Jesus the Christ. God so loved the world that he gave his only Son, so that everyone who believes in him may not perish but have eternal life.[162] That includes you and me, if we are willing to believe. So we can see.

What is breathtaking to me is recognizing what this simple statement really means. God came to us in the form of Jesus because he knew we could not make it on our own. In other words, we need Divine Mercy to grow into what God desperately wants us to become: fully alive human beings in the process of becoming one with our God, who is love eternal.

This is not some empty promise. There is overwhelming evidence that the human spirit, and as a result the whole human person, flourishes best in the nurturing environment of recognized and accepted unconditional love. Knowing that mistakes made are

---

160   MK 10: 51-52
161   JN: 4: 1-30
162   JN 3:16

only lessons learned, that everything belongs. Because it is in just such an environment that the human spirit feels empowered to risk becoming more.

What can we do about it?

It's as simple as this. We have a choice: God's mercy now or God's justice later. What do we miss when we fail to take advantage of God's mercy? In a very real sense, we miss everything.

Jesus coming back to talk about Divine Mercy is itself an example of God's mercy. It is an indication of how much he wants us to take advantage of this life-saving gift now. One that is ours with no strings attached. The only catch? It is our choice.

Jesus was clear about how we take advantage of this gift.

Whenever I want to improve my relationship with another, the surest way to so is by communicating with that person, expressing my honest feelings and listening to his or hers. When we try to open ourselves to God, when we try to improve our relationship with Jesus, we call this communication prayer. More about the general subject of prayer later. At this point let me comment on two prayer aids that relate specifically to Divine Mercy.

The first is known as the Divine Mercy Chaplet. Roughly similar to the Rosary, it is a meditative way to acknowledge our need for God's mercy that was revealed to Saint Faustina. If you would like more information, just Google the phrase "Divine Mercy Chaplet." I can tell you from personal experience that it is a grace-filled exercise when done with others.

The second prayer aid is an image of Jesus that also comes to us from Saint Faustina. According to her, Jesus gave specific instructions concerning the image so it could be used for veneration (which means to meditate on, treating with great respect). The image shows Jesus raising his right hand in a gesture of blessing and pointing with his left hand on his chest, from which flow forth two rays: one red and one white (translucent). The depiction often contains the message "Jesus, I trust in You!" (Polish: *Jezu ufam Tobie*). The rays streaming out have symbolic meaning: red for the blood of Jesus (which is the life of souls) and pale for the water (which justifies souls). The whole image is symbolic of the charity, forgiveness, and love of God, referred to as the "fountain of mercy."[163] Standing, sitting, or kneeling in front of this image and clearing one's mind is an excellent way to pray about God's mercy. Think of it as coming to Jesus with the certainty he is present to help.

---

163 Wikipedia, Divine Mercy image

For those of you uncomfortable with the whole idea of Jesus actually appearing to someone like Sister Faustina, I offer two thoughts. First, if our God is real, is really almighty, is truly love without condition, why not? Second, remember the little Jesuit test I suggested in our discussion of "Believe and You Will See." If I choose to believe and it helps me accept God's mercy, allowing me to experience more joy in my life, and then on my last day discover Jesus never appeared to Sister Faustina, what have I lost? If, on the other hand, I choose to not believe, and I continue to ignore God's mercy, and then on my last day discover Jesus' interactions with Sister Faustina were real, what have I lost? Once again, why not?

Asking for and trusting in God's mercy provides the foundation for becoming God's mercy to others. It still takes our willingness to use the graces God so freely gives us to become examples of his love to those we encounter. If your first reaction is that you are not adequately prepared to do this, remember God doesn't ask us to be prepared. He does not call the prepared, just the willing. Those willing to enter the chaos of others, on their terms, the only goal being their well-being.

The promise is this: as with all actions consistent with God's will, the one who benefits the most is the one who allows himself or herself to become an instrument of God's mercy. For, in the process, we become who we are. Remember?

It helps to start with the little things, for the habit of thinking of oneself as an example of God's mercy will then take root and grow. It's the way the whole idea of moral conscience works.

Our oldest daughter told me a story recently that helps make this point. She was busy shopping one day and encountered a former employee who was obviously distraught. It turned out she was unemployed, had just lost her wallet, and did not have the money to buy enough gas to drive home. Our daughter, at the time unemployed herself, gave her a hug, assured her things would get better, and then reached into her purse and gave her upset friend the only money she had, a twenty-dollar bill. Our daughter had entered the chaos of another, on that other person's terms, her only goal being that person's well-being. She told me the story because she was trying to understand why her simple act of kindness made her feel so good.

Actions that make us feel more whole lead to more far-reaching efforts on our part. Which make us feel more alive, more complete.

Which eventually makes the whole process seem second nature. It's the way we have been created.

My wife has always been a deeply caring person. Yet, I am still profoundly touched when I reflect on how she dealt with our friend Jeanne during the last ten to twelve years of Jeanne's life. As Jeanne aged, her various illnesses made her increasingly difficult to be with. Yet, each week my wife spent time with her: in person when we were close, by phone when we were distant. More often than not Jeanne was so preoccupied with her illnesses that she was downright unpleasant, and yet there was my wife, a smile on her face and love in her heart, helping Jeanne realize she was not alone, that someone cared. And guess who ended up feeling more loved?

If you would like a simple tool to help you focus on becoming an example of God's mercy, here is one I have found helpful. Just remember the words FROM, WITH, and FOR. When I feel an urge or inspiration to do something, where does this urge or inspiration come FROM? If it seems to have something to do with God's mercy, assume God has supplied the inspiration. Do whatever needs to be done, knowing you are doing so WITH God's grace. You and the Divine are doing this together. And when done, rejoice if you are able to feel you have done this FOR God, so others may know his love is real.

Finally, trust in the goodness of God's mercy. Simple idea, isn't it? So simple it is hard for us to grasp the potential benefits. I think this is true because trusting in God strikes at the heart of our desire to be our own god (original sin) and our tendency to think we are responsible for producing specific results (versus accepting we are only responsible for the effort). Yet, think of how freeing it would be if we could just learn to trust. That God is real. Is almighty. Is intimately involved in our lives. And will always lead us to new life when we trust in his goodness.

Would you not do the same for someone you loved unconditionally?

Real Presence

1 Corinthians 11:23–30; Mark 6:30–44; Mark 8:1–9; Mark 14:22–25; Matthew 26:26–30; Luke 24:13–35; John 6:1–71; John 13:1–17

At the beginning of this chapter, I asked that you read the referenced Scripture passage associated with each section before you start. Well, as I mentioned once before, there always seems to be an exception. For this chapter, you might find it more informative to read each Scripture passage when I first refer to it.

I would like to invite you to join me on a pilgrimage. It is a pilgrimage into the heart of the best example of God entering into our chaos, on our terms, his only objective our well-being.

We will cover sixty years in the fifteen or so minutes it takes for you to read this section. Our destination is a deeper understanding of the Eucharist. Catholic Christian doctrine proclaims the Eucharist is the source and summit of Christian living. Yet, a majority of Roman Catholics are indifferent to the Sacrament. And those who do spend time trying to understand what the phrase "Real Presence" means (that Jesus is truly present, body and blood, soul and divinity, in the consecrated bread and wine) often find themselves thinking, "This teaching is difficult. Who can believe it?" So the goal of our journey will be to answer two questions:

Where did the belief in Real Presence come from?

If Real Presence is true, why isn't it more obvious?

Our journey will use the New Testament and is made possible by an often overlooked trait of Scripture. While we are all aware that Holy Scripture is based on God's revelation, most of us do not realize it also provides a historical record of what was believed at the time any specific piece of scripture was written. This record reveals that acceptance of God's revelation takes time. This makes sense to me, because we humans have a tendency to cling to past beliefs. I think it has something to do with our resistance to change.

Two examples may help illustrate the lag time between God's revelation and human acceptance. It took over eight hundred years for a definitive written record to emerge concerning Moses, and then there was not one account but three, which were merged over the next four hundred years into a generally accepted set of stories. I am not saying there were no beliefs concerning Moses during those twelve hundred years. I am saying it took this long for there to be one accepted view that was generally believed. In the case of Jesus, it took over four hundred years for Christians to agree on who he was: true

God and true man. The Gospels themselves present different and evolving views of God's revelation concerning Jesus, representing different and evolving beliefs at the time these documents were written. But it took centuries of debate and discernment to realize the magnitude of God's gift. Interestingly, we will find on our journey that it took a comparatively brief period of only sixty years after Jesus' death for belief in the Real Presence to take root.

The first stop on our trip is Corinth, Greece, sometime around 50 AD. Jesus has been dead for approximately twenty years. A believer named Paul has come here to start a new community of Jesus followers, known as Followers of the Way. Previously pagan, these converts are attracted by Paul's claim that Jesus' resurrection from the dead means that all those who believe in him as the Christ (anointed one) of God can experience the same rebirth to everlasting life.

Unfortunately, they have a difficult time discerning what is truly important in their new religion. Specifically, there is a tendency for discourteous behavior, even drunkenness, during the Sunday morning communal meal that follows the Saturday evening reading of Scripture. Paul sends them a letter in which, among other things, he tells them the story of what Jesus did with bread and wine at the Last Supper. This is the first written record of what we refer to as the "words of institution." Paul's basic point is the Sunday morning communal meals are based on what Jesus said and must be taken seriously. He even attributes recent illness and deaths to a failure to do so.

Obviously, belief in Real Presence is not yet fully developed at this time. However, two important steps are being taken in that direction. What Jesus said and did at the Last Supper is clearly the heart of early forms of worship among those choosing to follow Jesus. In addition, Paul's account notes that Jesus blessed (gave thanks for) the bread and wine before offering it to his apostles. The Gospels were all written in Greek, and the Greek word for blessing (giving thanks for) is *eucharistia*. All Scripture mentions of what we call Eucharist include this reference. Think of it as a key to Gospel passages concerning Eucharist, and the earliest place we find it in the New Testament is in Paul's first letter to the Corinthians.

Our next stop occurs some fifteen to twenty years later, around 70 AD. An unknown author writing for a Greek-speaking community of Gentile believers introduces the first written record of Jesus' life. This remarkable document is the Gospel according to Mark. Included are the "words of institution" from the Last Supper. They are slightly different from, but similar in spirit to, Paul's account. In addition, Mark includes a story so significant to his community that he tells it twice as two similar but separate incidents, in Chapter 6 and Chapter 8. We know this story as the "multiplication of loaves and fishes."

In both cases, Jesus is able miraculously to feed thousands. Bread is involved and clearly takes center stage in the second telling of the story, with Jesus blessing the bread before the food is distributed. There is growing belief in Jesus' ability to transform bread into a new kind of food for his followers.

Approximately ten years later, around 80 to 85 AD, another unknown author who chooses the name Matthew writes his version of Jesus' life. This author has access to Mark's Gospel but also material gleaned from other sources. He is intent on presenting Jesus as the fulfillment of Jewish Scripture because he is writing for a largely Jewish community of Jesus followers. The Last Supper and the multiplication of loaves and fishes are featured, both including the important references to Jesus giving thanks for, or blessing, the elements to be distributed. What is most striking, however, are the actual "words of institution" in Matthew's Gospel. There is a much stronger invitation to eat and drink, signifying the growing belief that this is Jesus himself who is being shared. In addition, the cadence and rhythm of the words (not too dissimilar from what we use today) indicate a more fully developed and standardized form of worship. The seed of God's revelation is bearing fruit.

Our pilgrimage now moves forward about another ten years, to around 90 AD. A highly educated Gentile Greek Christian, who chooses the name Luke, produces his Gospel (and what we know as the Acts of the Apostles) for a community of Gentile Greek Christians. His message of Jesus coming to save all peoples is based primarily on Mark, another independent source also used by Matthew, and material of his own.

Luke includes the multiplication of loaves and fishes and the "words of institution" at the Last Supper in his Gospel. He also adds one new story that is critical to our pilgrimage. This is the story of two disciples walking from Jerusalem to Emmaus the first Sunday after Jesus' crucifixion.

An allegory is a story that contains another story of deeper and more pervasive importance. The "Road to Emmaus" story is an allegory. Superficially, we have a story of two disciples walking to Emmaus. Jesus joins them. The disciples do not recognize Jesus even though their hearts burn with excitement when Jesus discusses Scripture passages explaining why the Messiah had to suffer and die before entering into his glory. On reaching the village, the disciples ask Jesus to join them for dinner. During the meal, Jesus blesses and breaks bread, offering it to them to eat. As this happens, the disciples recognize Jesus, realizing he is really present in their midst. Jesus then disappears, and the disciples rush back to Jerusalem to share their good news with other disciples.

At a deeper level, the "Road to Emmaus" is also a description of Christian worship toward the end of the first century. The community first listened to and reflected on Scripture passages that dealt with the reasons for Jesus' suffering and death before his resurrection. Today we would call this the Liturgy of the Word. Then there would be a communal meal, which increasingly became a ceremonial meal centered on the Last Supper. During this meal, people became convinced Jesus was truly raised from the dead because he was really present in the consecrated bread and wine. He was in their midst. Today we call this the Liturgy of the Eucharist. Together, the Liturgies of the Word and Eucharist represent what we call the Mass, during which we celebrate Jesus' presence in the community (two disciples on a journey), Scripture (were not our hearts burning?), and, in a tangible way, the Eucharist (he was made known to them in the breaking of the bread).

This interpretation of the "Road to Emmaus" story helps explain why belief in the risen Jesus spread so quickly. Too often we attribute this solely to stories of his appearances to the Apostles. But how quickly would you accept such stories when told by a small number of men who had nothing to lose and everything to gain from the acceptance of their stories? When you add the power of knowing Jesus' Real Presence at community worship to these stories, the almost miraculous spread of belief in the risen Lord makes much more sense.

So, just sixty years after Jesus' death, we have the answer to "Where did the belief in Real Presence come from?" It came from the lives of early Christian believers. This belief was so ingrained in the worship practices of early Christians that it took another eight hundred years before the Church hierarchy felt it was necessary to publish a formal doctrine with words like "transubstantiation."

The answer to our second question, "If Real Presence is true, why isn't it more obvious?" requires one last stop on our pilgrimage. We don't even have to move forward in time, for during the same period as Luke's Gospel appears, a fourth account of Jesus life, known as the Gospel of John, is completed. Most probably written by several authors within the Community of the Apostle John's followers (known as the Johannine Community), the sources of this Gospel are also unknown. Most biblical scholars believe that one important source was either John himself or another disciple who had accompanied Jesus during his public ministry.

The Gospel of John differs in important ways from the first three Gospels. The most important difference lies in John's assertion that Jesus was divine before his birth because he is the Divine Word (Logos) of God. There are other differences, but for our purposes the most significant is how John chooses to deal with the Eucharist. John's version of the Last Supper makes no mention of Jesus blessing bread and wine and then saying the "words of institution." The Gospel author is able to do this because he has previously devoted an entire chapter, Chapter 6, to the subject of Real Presence in the Eucharist.

Chapter 6 begins with the story of multiplication of loaves and fishes. The crowd is so impressed they want to make Jesus their King. Realizing their intent, Jesus leaves to go off by himself. That night, his disciples are caught in a serious storm on the Sea of Galilee and are saved only when Jesus comes walking on the water to aid them.

The next day, the crowd finds Jesus in Capernaum, and a long dialogue ensues. During this dialogue, Jesus confirms the reality of Real Presence by saying he is the bread of life, that those who eat his flesh and drink his blood gain eternal life because his flesh is real food and his blood real drink. Furthermore, whoever eats this flesh and drinks this blood abides in Jesus as he abides in them. Jesus concludes by saying that whoever eats this bread will live forever. [164]

To which some of his disciples, who as recently as the day before were his loyal followers, some of whom may have been saved by Jesus from the previous night's storm, say, "This teaching is difficult. Who can accept it?"[165]

The first reason Real Presence is not more obvious is, as in all things, that we have free will. We can choose to believe or not believe. Once again, some things, especially matters of the heart and of the Spirit, must be believed before they can be seen. We must be willing

164   JN 6:35, 53-58
165   JN 6:60

to decide we believe, letting our experience validate or invalidate our decision. The Real Presence is real to an individual only when there is a decision to believe. Think of it as our willingness to be present to the Real Presence. For many reasons, some born of doubt, some born of indifference, far too may Catholic Christians' entire thought process regarding Real Presence can be summarized as, "This teaching is difficult. Who can accept it?"

Think of the opportunity missed! For what reason?

The second reason Real Presence is not more obvious can be found in the story John chooses to tell in his account of the Last Supper. Modern-day readers have a hard time understanding just how shocked Jesus' apostles must have been when it became apparent Jesus intended to wash their feet. Most people in first-century Israel went barefooted or wore sandals. The job of washing another's feet was reserved for the lowest, most detested slave. No wonder Peter initially refused to participate! And yet, this is what Jesus did, washing his apostles feet as the lowest, most detested slave would do. And then he said, "I have set you an example, that you also should do as I have done for you."[166] You should become me to others. You should become my Real Presence by serving others.

John was telling us something very important: there is a synergistic relationship between consuming the Real Presence in the Eucharist and our willingness to use our gifts to serve others. "Synergistic" means each element becomes more in union with another. Eucharist gives us the graces to serve more compassionately, and sharing ourselves with others adds greater depth and richness to our appreciation of the Eucharist, allowing us to experience more fully the deep of joy of Christ's presence within us. Pope Benedict XVI provides an especially compelling description of this phenomenon in his first Encyclical, "Deus Caritas Est."[167] In fact, he goes on to say, "If in my life I fail completely to heed others, solely out of a desire to be 'devout' and to perform my 'religious duties,' then my relationship with God will also grow arid. It becomes merely 'proper,' but loveless. Only my readiness to encounter my neighbor and to show him love makes me sensitive to God as well."[168]

---

166   JN 13:15
167   *Deus Caritas Est*, Pope Benedict XVI, 14
168   *Deus Caritas Est*, Pope Benedict XVI, 18

The true significance of the Eucharist becomes more obvious whenever we who receive it are willing to become Christ to one another. "For love grows through love."[169]

Imagine for a moment:

What would happen
if just those who profess belief in the Real Presence
were to follow John's teaching?

Imagine
the impact on those who doubt,
or those mired in indifference,
starving spiritually,
so in need of someone to touch them,
so they too will recognize
the Real Presence of Jesus.

---

169   *Deus Caritas Est*, Pope Benedict XVI, 18

Reconciliation

Luke 15:11–32, John 20:19–23

Greg used to be the organist at a Parish I belong to in New Hampshire. He was a great asset for more years than I care to count and was always a pleasure to work with. At least until the day I mentioned in a homily that God's forgiveness is unconditional.

I stated God's love is unconditional. Therefore, his forgiveness must also be unconditional. Greg sent me an email disagreeing, and we have had a friendly back-and-forth ever since. Greg argues we must seek God's forgiveness for it to be operative in our lives. That's a condition. I agree God's forgiveness is like any of his gifts. We must be willing to accept them. However, I do not think that changes the unconditional offering of the gift. Obviously, the same point can be made about any form of God's love: the gift must be accepted, opened, and used for the receiver to realize the benefits of the gift. I am not sure I will ever convince Greg, but as with most things I am forced to spend time thinking about, I am a better person for the discussion we have had.

Forgiveness is important. It frees us from harmful emotions like unhealthy guilt and shame and allows us to fully engage in life. We all need forgiveness because we all make mistakes. We all sin. Sin involves our decisions to abuse one or more of God's gifts. All conscious choices to abuse God's gifts separate us in relationship: from ourselves, loved ones, acquaintances, and God. Since relationships are the source of all emotional growth, we become less when we sin. This is the reason God detests sin. We need forgiveness to shed the emotional and spiritual shackles resulting from sin so we can grow and become more.

Anyone familiar with Roman Catholic education, particularly prior to Vatican II, is familiar with the terms "venial sin" and "mortal sin." It seemed to me while in Catholic grade school that venial sin was not that important and almost everything else was a mortal sin. Missing Mass on Sunday or a Holy Day, any kind of sexual act, disobedience of Church teaching (which often translated to disobeying the nuns teaching our classes) all appeared to carry the threat of everlasting damnation.

A favorite book of mine for returning Catholics is *Good Goats, Healing Our Image of God* by Dennis, Sheila, and Matthew Linn. The first chapter is entitled "Good Old Uncle George."[170] In it a loving

---

170   *Healing Our Image of God,* Dennis, Sheila and Matthew Linn, p. 3

father and mother take their child to visit good old Uncle George, who lives in a large mansion. Uncle George greets the family, gruffly explains he expects to see them at least once a week, shows them around his largely dark and forbidding home, and concludes his tour by leading them down into the basement. The youngster can see the flames and hear the unearthly screams. Uncle George informs him that this is where he will almost certainly go if he fails to visit Uncle George every week. On the drive home after the visit, the Mother says to her child, "And now don't you love Uncle George with all your heart and soul, mind and strength?[171]"

Vatican II did much good for many reasons, just one of which was clarifying the concepts of venial and mortal sin. All sin should be taken seriously because all sin weakens us, makes us less, and, when not dealt with, predisposes us to more serious sin. Venial sin wounds us spiritually, weakening our relationships. Mortal sin kills us spiritually because mortal sin involves only grave matters when we have full knowledge of what we are doing and proceed with deliberate consent.[172] Killing someone is an example of a grave matter. In other words, mortal sin is possible (our free will), is limited to only *extremely* grave matters when we understand what we are doing and go ahead anyway, and is so serious because it severs our relationship with God and others.

Because our God is a loving God, four of the seven Sacraments of our Church deal with forgiveness of sins. Baptism is the first and chief Sacrament of forgiveness because it unites us with Christ.[173] Anointing of the Sick, available to all who need healing or are facing death, also features forgiveness of sin. The Eucharist includes graces that wipe away venial sin. But the primary Sacrament for dealing with all sin in our daily lives is the Sacrament of Reconciliation.

For centuries this Sacrament was referred to as Penance or Confession. As part of the Vatican II changes instituted in the 1960s, the Sacrament name was changed to Reconciliation. Today we tend to use the names interchangeably. Penance and Confession imply that the primary undertaking in the Sacrament is our effort to admit and atone for our sins. Reconciliation implies that the primary power in the Sacrament is God helping us return to relationship with him. I like the idea of Reconciliation.

---

171 *Healing Our Image of God,* Dennis, Shelia and Matthew Linn, P. 3
172 Catechism, 1855, 1857
173 Catechism, 977

The parable of the prodigal son helps us understand several things about Reconciliation.

The younger son and the older son both sin. They choose to separate themselves from the father who loves them dearly. As a result, both become less: the younger son destitute and starving, the older son unable to join the celebration. Both need to be reconciled with the father.

Reconciliation requires a decision. The father has already made his. He is longing for his sons' return, anxiously waiting, running to embrace one of them, reminding the other, "All that is mine is yours."[174] The younger son, mired in his poverty and hunger, decides to return to the father. He travels home, confesses the mistakes he has made, and acknowledges his sorrow by offering to atone for his sins. As a result, he ends up in the celebration prepared for him by his father. The older son decides to rebuff his father's attempt to be reconciled. His decision leaves him mired in his resentment and false pride. As a result, the story ends with the older son unable to join the celebration.

The Sacrament of Reconciliation is like any gift. We must accept it to realize its benefits. Like the younger son, we must decide to get up and go to the Father. Like the younger son, we must then be willing to confess our sins, express our sorrow, and atone for our sins. The Church calls these three actions confession, contrition, and satisfaction.[175] They represent our half of the Sacrament of Reconciliation.

The other half involves God's actions through the priest. These include forgiving our sins and giving us the graces needed to accept forgiveness; to know freedom from destructive shame, guilt, or remorse; and to rebuild the way we view ourselves as well restore relationships with others and our God.

Unfortunately, the Sacrament of Reconciliation is ignored by a majority of Catholics. Over the years I have been given three reasons for this phenomenon:

---

174   LK 15:31
175   Catechism, 1448

1. *If I go to Confession, everyone will know I am a sinner.*

Guess what, we all are. Trying to pretend you aren't puts you in the company of the older son, mired in resentment and/or false pride and missing the celebration.

2. *If I go to Confession, and I am honest, the priest will think less of me.*

I have had the privilege of being a permanent deacon for twenty-five years. Permanent deacons are not supposed to hear confessions. Yet, I have heard many (the non-sacramental kind, of course), some from priests wanting to unburden themselves. I have never heard a priest, in ANY circumstance, say anything negative about what he has heard in the confessional. What I have heard, from several priests, is how rewarding it is to participate in the Sacrament with someone making the effort to be as honest and genuine as possible.

3. *I don't remember or know what to say.*

Don't laugh. This is a very common concern. The answer is simple. When you enter the confessional, just say your first name (if you don't know the priest), tell him it has been a long time since you took advantage of this Sacrament, and ask him to help you. I can almost guarantee you will be pleasantly surprised.

Of course, when we get through these concerns, two underlying causes tend to surface. The more common is apathy or indifference. "I simply haven't given it much thought." "What good would it do me? I'm doing all right." "You don't understand; I'm busy." Those who think this way haven't been willing to obey, meaning to listen to and understand in faith (remember the definition from "On Being Human"?). When we think this way, we are declaring that we do not need God's mercy, or we can't bring ourselves to accept that God's mercy is real. We become the older son.

A few people have actually given the matter a fair amount of thought and challenge the whole idea of the Sacrament. Who says the priest is the only one who can forgive? Who says God works through the priest? Why can't I just talk to God directly? Does it really make that much difference?

Who says the priest is the only one who can forgive?

No one I know. Every priest I have ever known has encouraged people to be forgiving. Jesus taught (and psychologists confirm) that we know forgiveness as we forgive.[176] Forgiving increases our sense of well-being, even our overall health. Going to the Sacrament of Reconciliation without being willing to forgive others is an empty gesture, for "If I speak without love, I am no more than a gong booming or a cymbal clashing."[177]

With this all said, the distinction drawn by our Church concerns forgiveness of sins. Sin, by its very nature, damages our self-esteem (relationship with self) as well as our relationships with others (in Roman Catholic terms, the Body of Christ) and with God. When we forgive another, we are dealing with an offense affecting us. This is what gives us the power and right to forgive. How can any person offer forgiveness for all those (other than himself or herself) affected by the sin? How can any person forgive for God?

Our Church teaches that only God forgives sin.[178] Even though God's forgiveness is unconditional, God must speak for himself. How you would feel if, when offended by another, you decided to forgive but were never given an opportunity to express your forgiveness to the offender? The answer is that the forgiveness would be empty of its real potential for healing. It's why the Sacrament should be called Reconciliation.

Our Church also teaches that in the Sacrament of Reconciliation, God has given the priest the grace to act as an intermediary for God and the entire Body of Christ. This belief goes all the way back to the idea of Apostolic Succession (Christ chose and gave special graces to his Apostles, who subsequently passed these graces on to their successors, all the way down to our current priests.) I like the idea of being able to go to one person rather than the entire Body of Christ when I want to be forgiven.

Who says only priests can forgive? No one. Who says only God can forgive sin? The Faith Traditions of every Christian, Jew, and Muslim. Who says that only a priest can act as an intermediary for God in the forgiveness of sins? The Roman Catholic Church.

Who says God works through the priest?

Scripture as understood by Roman Catholicism. In the twentieth chapter of John's Gospel, the risen Jesus comes to the frightened

---

176   *Scattered Raindrops*, Deacon Bill Rich, p.39
177   1st Corinthians 13: 1
178   Catechism, 1441

Apostles in a locked room, says "Peace be with you"[179] twice, and then says, "As the Father has sent me, so I am sending you.... Receive the Holy Spirit. If you forgive the sins of any, they are forgiven them; if you retain the sins of any, they are retained."[180]

Our Church believes the Holy Spirit is actively involved in the forgiveness of sins, acting through the priest, who as an assistant to the bishop shares in the graces transmitted from the earliest Apostles. The Holy Spirit is also active in us, working through our conscience to lead us to seek forgiveness, and present in the graces we receive when we participate in the Sacrament of Reconciliation. I will never forget a beautiful account of the prodigal son parable I read once (so long ago I can't remember where). In it the author described God's mercy extending to the Holy Spirit giving the younger son the strength to return to the Father. God's mercy is so great it even extends to helping us seek it. I am touched every time I think of this.

Other Christian faith traditions will argue that Christ gave the power to forgive sins on his behalf to all Christian believers. I respect their right to do so. I also think the systemic cause for this view is not so much real differences of opinion today as a centuries-old desire to create distance from the notion of Apostolic Succession tied to a Papacy responsible for perceived (and in some cases real) abuses.

I am sure it is because of my upbringing, but I like the idea of a formal Sacrament that requires me to go to the Father, confess my sins, express my sorrow, and seek atonement for my sins. I have never regretted doing so. I have often felt much better. I feel at one with the prodigal son. I like celebrating.

Why can't I talk to God directly?

You can and are encouraged to do so. But the prodigal son had to get up and go to his father to ask for forgiveness before he could take part in the celebration. I think making this kind of effort is part of the process that allows us to accept God's forgiveness. Besides, talking directly to God still leaves you with the problem of reaching every other member of the Body of Christ.

Does it really make that much difference?

I leave this one to you. Remember: Doubt is helpful as long as you deal with it. You will become stronger in the process.

My own belief is this: Taking advantage of the Sacrament of Reconciliation helps me grow in humility and peace of mind. It is

179   JN 20: 20-21
180   JN 20: 21-23

also essential to my ability to experience the joy that flows from responding to God's call to reconciliation.

In the end, if you choose to believe in the Sacrament of Reconciliation and learn in the next life that it was a fiction, what have you lost? If, because of indifference or conscious choice, you choose to believe the Sacrament of Reconciliation is a fiction, and in the end it turns out to be true, what have you lost? If the answers are almost nothing and a lot, why not?

Body of Christ

Romans 12:2–8

On a cool but sunny autumn afternoon in early December 1989, I was told I had prostate cancer. My doctor of many years, Art D'Souza, had discovered it in a routine physical exam, and it had been confirmed in a biopsy. As soon as we could, we went to see the urologist to explore potential treatments. In response to my request to be as direct and candid as possible about my future, the urologist told me the odds were I would be dead in seven to eight years. Apparently I had a particularly virulent form of prostate cancer.

Three months later, after much discussion and debate, I had my prostate surgically removed (the procedure, though very common today, was just leaving the experimental stage back then). Obviously, I am very much alive today, over twenty years later. But I will never forget the lessons I learned going through that initial experience. There were many, most of which I won't bore you with, but I would like to share two with you.

The first sets the stage for the second. I decided to stop doing things that added no value to my life. I wanted to spend whatever time I had left on those things that gave me joy. Naturally, there are small things in everyone's life that must be done, but, as I proudly announced to my wife, I no longer had the luxury of enduring bad days. If I was doing something I thought a waste of time, I stopped. If I was spending time with people who detracted from my life, I stopped. People I used to pretend were important to me, or people I thought I just HAD to put up with, slowly faded into insignificance. People and activities that stimulated me in positive ways, helping me feel a greater sense of connectedness to life, slowly became more prominent in my life. Writing *Scattered Raindrops* and this book are but two examples.

I wanted to treat my remaining time for what it was: the precious present (as in the here and now) and the precious present (as in gift). I wanted to maximize what is most important to me.

Former business acquaintances have all but disappeared from my life. Activities that used to take so much time (like consulting work, golf, large parties, attending meetings without purpose) are largely a thing of the past. My diaconate work, painting, writing, fly-fishing, visiting grandchildren, and traveling with my wife have become more prominent. Yes, my wife gets irritated from time to time for what she claims is my lack of interest (guilty) or forgetfulness (guilty). There are also times my wife has to insist I simply MUST do something, but that does not happen often. Because she is one of the people who give me joy.

After I had been on this adventure for some months, I discovered the obvious, which is the second lesson I would like to share.

All the important things in my life are grounded in my relationships. I love fly-fishing, but not nearly so much when faced with fishing by myself. Painting and writing are primarily solitary activities, but for me they are also ways to share myself with others. Even my centering prayer each day, done in complete silence, involves relationship, in this case with the Divine. Those I love and who love me in return help me grow. They bring color and texture to my life. They are helping me find my way home.

The advantage of having cancer is it has forced me to break through all the protective barriers I had built up over my life. I retired early (at age fifty-two, almost twenty years ago) to ensure I could spend whatever remaining time I had on things important to me. I tell people I love that I love them more often. I say thank you more often to people who have helped me or who have just made me feel better. I have found it easier to feel compassion. As a result, I have become more sensitive to the needs of those I encounter; I listen better; I find it easier to share what I am feeling.

Somewhere along the way, I discovered I had stumbled on the great gift called the Body of Christ.

The Body of Christ was first conceived of and articulated by St. Paul in his letter to the Romans. He was asking the followers of Jesus to set aside their selfish interests, their protective barriers, and allow themselves to be transformed (changed in a fundamental way) by the power the Holy Spirit, so they could work together as one family. To do so, they had to accept all members as important because all had unique gifts that would help the entire community, or "body," grow and become more. They also had to accept that only Christ was the true head of this body.

Think of the power of this idea. When one person succeeds, all succeed. When one person suffers, all suffer. When one believer is transformed by sharing his or her gifts, others are touched. So that, one encounter at a time, Christ becomes more present. Church congregations can be transformed into more vibrant worship communities. And participants in that transformation find they can lead more meaningful lives.

What a gift, made possible by the action of the Holy Spirit. Available when we are willing to set aside our selfish interests, open ourselves to using our gifts to engage with others, so that we, and whatever family is important to us, can live life more fully.

The phrase "Body of Christ" is often applied to all who belong to our Church, or our faith tradition. Sometimes it is called the mystical (meaning spiritual) Body of Christ. At times it is also used to refer to just the laity. In fact, the phrase literally means all who belong to the greater (meaning larger) catholic (meaning universal) Christian Church, meaning all those who call themselves Christian and have been baptized.[181]

Some use the term "People of God" in place of "Body of Christ." While there are theological differences in the two terms, the idea behind both is very similar. The Church is us. Called by God to join in community to love as he has loved us, to accept each other despite our superficial differences, to struggle with the weaknesses we all have, relying on each other's strengths, so we can find our way home...together. It is not just what some other religion, the Vatican, some bishop, or some priest does. It is what we all do. Including you and me. Together. For church, whether among friends and family or any broader categorization, is always community. There is no church without community. We become more, or less, together.

I pray for the time when all who claim to be People of God, or members of the Body of Christ (baptized Christians), or just all who claim they want to more joy in life, will spend more time setting aside selfish interests to share, forgive, and care. So that we all can be transformed into more viable and vibrant communities.

Some of you may wonder why I have chosen to limit myself to the Body of Christ. Why not everyone? The answer is this: I grow the most and I am able to contribute the most when I:

- focus on my Parish family,
- within the structure of a Church that teaches (even though, like me, it does not always practice) the values I believe are the pathway to eternal life,
- and is empowered and led by a power greater than myself, whom I choose to call Jesus.

I firmly believe transformation happens one person at a time, within a setting that by its example demonstrates the benefits of such change. Several examples may help make this point.

181   Catechism, 817, 818

One evening many years ago, our friend Father Dave Riley told Frannie and me about his dream. He wanted to take unneeded clothing from the affluent area we lived in (Ridgefield, Connecticut) to a nun he knew in Appalachia. He couldn't because there was no way to transport the clothing. Without thinking, I promised to find him as many trucks as he could fill (I was still drinking back then). And so our adventure began.

It seemed as if the whole Parish pitched in. Some five months later, a slew of people loaded five large rented trucks to the gills. And off we went: five drivers, five backup drivers, and, on each of the four trips we made, one of my children.

I am sure the people in Appalachia benefited from the clothing, toys, and other assorted items we brought. But the real beneficiaries were those of us who had solicited the goods, had them cleaned and packed in boxes, loaded them into trucks, and then drove those trucks to and from Appalachia. We had done it together. And every one of us was changed by the experience. Just ask any of my kids.

I have already described Frannie's Baptism after an eighteen-year journey ("Importance of the Journey"). What I didn't mention is how the journey started and how it ended. Frannie did not decide one day to become Catholic. She didn't even start her journey by deciding to investigate Catholicism. She just thought singing in the church choir might be fun. She was welcomed with open arms, and so, without really deciding to do so, she became part of our Parish community. Eventually, she decided to try and convert. For years she took classes and studied with different priests. I think she just wore them out, with the exception of Father Dave Riley, who simply wouldn't give up.

About this time, we were forming the team to do our second teen retreat in the spring of 1981. Frannie announced she and our friend Jeanne were joining the team because they knew I needed help. For almost two months they came to our team meetings. Frannie listened to talks, helped surmount the inevitable roadblocks to a successful retreat, laughed, cried, and felt overwhelmed, all with other members of our team.

At the Sunday Mass on that retreat, Frannie slowly but steadily walked up to Father Charlie during Communion and extended her hand. With tears in his eyes, Father Charlie gave her a host. Frannie had found home. Years of trying to think and pray her way into belief gave way to the lived experience of being part of a community whose only purpose was sharing with others the reality of a loving God.

Frannie and I have continued to lead similar retreats for adults in almost every Parish we have joined. I could tell you great stories from each one. There is something amazing about a group of individuals coming together, setting aside their own agendas, and focusing on how to share with others. It borders on the miraculous. At the beginning, the goal seems almost impossible. As the inevitable problems come up, the temptation grows to over-control, or argue, or settle for less. And yet, if the team can just trust in the goodness of God, with each member making the effort to do his or her part, the results are ALWAYS breathtaking. And the ones who gain the most are not those who attend the retreat, but those on the team who have given the most, who have made the Body of Christ real.

When asked one day by a friend what I would do if I learned I had only six months to live, I replied without hesitating. I would like to be part of one more retreat team.

There are countless other examples of being transformed by the action of the local Body of Christ. When I had the operation to remove my prostate, another friend, Father David Blanchfield, and a group of parishioners celebrated Mass while I was in the operating room. I have never felt such peace. I will never forget the feeling of belonging I felt at Frannie's Baptism and my Mass of Thanksgiving following my ordination, the comfort I experienced at my father's Memorial Mass, the sense of being at one with others present at almost every funeral I attend. I actually tear up every time my friend Father Edmund, pastor of two New Hampshire Parishes, in the midst of dealing with his newest problem, catches himself, smiles his big smile and asks, "So, how's Frannie?" I could go on, but let me finish with one last example, one I recently witnessed.

Jimmy, who has had a hard time with life, came to live with his grandparents in New Hampshire this past summer. When I first met him, he appeared downcast and communicated in sullen one-word responses. His grandfather, a daily Mass attendee and active participant in Parish activities, started taking Jim with him everywhere, including Mass each day. Not too many weeks later I encountered a new Jimmy, full of life and eager to interact. He helped distribute songbooks before Mass, and with his grandfather watered the new flowers afterwards. He seemed to know and get along with everyone. During Mass, I happened to look over toward Jimmy during the Our Father, and there he was praying, arms outstretched, holding his grandfather's hand on his right and another parishioner's on his left, a smile of his face. I know his grandfather and grandmother are primarily responsible for bringing Jimmy back to life. However, the ability to do so within a Parish family environment helped make that transformation possible. I also know that seeing another human able to change with the support of others has helped me.

There are two Traditions within our Church that make the Body of Christ even more special. Both are covered in the Creed we say each weekend. The first is the idea of the communion of saints. The second is the resurrection of the body with life everlasting.

When we say "communion of saints," we are expanding the Body of Christ to include all those who have gone before us and are now saints. A saint is anyone who has left this life and is now is heaven.[182] This means all those in heaven are part of our community, available as intercessors (to intervene on our behalf) and confidants. It also means we will see them again, including dearly loved ones who have passed from this life.

When we talk about heaven, it may help some to spend just a moment on the ideas of hell and purgatory. Much is made of hell and eternal damnation by some Christian faith traditions (including ours in centuries past). The reality is this: there can be no heaven without a hell. If we are given free will, there must be a choice. And all choices have consequences.

No one knows what hell is like. No one is even certain if anyone is there. Jesus referred to it as a garbage dump (Gehenna was a garbage dump near Jerusalem). Because there are several references to unquenchable fire in both Hebrew and Christian Scriptures, popular images of hell include everlasting fire. There is no doubt in my mind in my mind there is a hell, meaning some alternative to union with the Divine. I don't know what it is like (at times, when I am feeling lonely, I imagine it as everlasting separation from all relationships). I do know I never want to find out.

Purgatory is one of our Traditions. While often spoken of in negative terms, it should be a cause for hope.[183] The whole idea of purgatory is to prepare us for everlasting union with the Divine by completing the process of making us whole. While fire has been associated with this undertaking, there have also been suggestions that it is a peaceful transition. Personally, I like Pope Benedict's description of purgatory as the transforming encounter with the Living Christ.[184]

---

182   Catechism, p. 898
183   *Spe Salvi Encyclical,* Pope Benedict XVI, 45 – 47
184   *Spe Salvi,* Pope Benedict XVI, 47

Resurrection of the body with life everlasting adds still another dimension to the Body of Christ. The idea is profound. When time ends and Jesus returns for the final judgment, all those in heaven or who are destined for heaven will be reunited with their earthly bodies, freed from all imperfection. These elect will then live on this earth (made whole) forever, meaning life without end.

These two ideas, communion of saints and resurrection of the dead with life everlasting, mean that the Body of Christ, imperfect and struggling to grow in meaningful ways today, transcends both space and time. And we will be with those we cherish, forever. How's that for joyful living?

Sound too far farfetched? Too good to be true? I think it is but one example of our inability to fully grasp the depth and breadth of God's infinite mercy and unconditional love. I choose to believe it. I have nothing to lose and everything to gain. Because if this is not God's plan, I know something better is.

The Body of Christ:
A gift freely given.

When opened,
we become
one (meaning connected in love),
holy (made whole),
Catholic (universal),
and apostolic (living the values we espouse)
Church (family).
Amen (so be it).

Scripture

John 3:16–17

My introduction to Holy Scripture, or the Bible, came relatively late in life. When I entered the permanent diaconate formation program at age forty-four, I had only a passing familiarity with the Bible. As with most Catholics of my generation, what I did know had come from primary school religion classes, the Baltimore Catechism, and the Sunday Mass readings. This did not trouble me. I assumed I knew what I needed to know. To tell the truth, I didn't think of the Bible as terribly relevant. Why keep repeating the same old stories, particularly when we didn't even know if some of them were true? More than once I thought to myself that we needed more current stories about God to make him relevant.

With this mindset, imagine my surprise as I first started studying Scripture as part of my diaconate training. Intellectual curiosity was soon replaced by a growing fascination with what I was studying. I became so absorbed I started short-changing work and my family. I couldn't get enough of it. When asked by my wife to explain what was happening, I told her I felt like someone dying of thirst in the desert who had just discovered an oasis overflowing with water.

I now know that part of this initial crush was a dedicated professor, Dr. Donald Gray, who had a wonderful way of engaging both mind and heart in his teaching. I had the privilege of studying under Don for three full years during my diaconate training program.

I have also come to realize that the Bible is like all of God's gifts. It will always give us more than we expect when we make a sincere effort to use it. In my case, the Bible has helped me know more intimately the God beyond my understanding. It has helped me experience more intensely the wonder of his love, and it has helped me see his presence more clearly in my own life. By taking the time to understand what had seemed to be outdated stories, I now know they are timeless in their truth. I also know that in many ways I myself have become a more current version of their telling.

The Bible contains the epic account of God creating everything, calling a people to himself, and then entering human history, all to share his love. As such, it is a love story. This love story is grounded in relationships: God's efforts to help his loved ones come into right relationship with him and each other. These struggles contain tragedy, romance, mystery, and adventure told through a collection of stories, songs, and sayings inspired by the Holy Spirit over two millennia. Above all, the Bible is the saga of God's enduring and unconditional love in the face of stumbling and often unsuccessful responses on the part of those loved. The Bible gives us insights into our nature and the nature of God. These insights help us to experience the reality of God's love and to grow through more loving relationships with one another.

The story begins with the one true God who loves more passionately than a lover,[185] a bridegroom,[186] a husband and father,[187] or a mother.[188] This one God creates all there is in love. He chooses to be intimately involved in his creation because he wants to be known; he wants to be loved in return. He gives man and woman free will so they have the capacity to do so.

God is a promise maker. Repeatedly, he vows to protect and care for those he has created in his own image so long as they are willing to love in return. He even promises to lead them to unimagined joy, called the Promised Land.[189]

Usually, these promises are called "covenants," a term referring to the most common form of contractual agreement in the ancient Middle East. Two things are often missed in a discussion of these covenants. First, and most importantly, God never gives up on those he loves. Despite repeated failures on our part to respond, God always find a way to try again. This is one of the points Jesus was making when he told the parable of the farmer who sowed his precious seed everywhere.[190] In his love, God continues to reach out to us wherever we are.

The other point often missed is that all God's promises contain the opportunity to live life more fully. The Exodus story, with God leading his loved ones out of slavery to the Promised Land, is present in every offer of God's love. God is always trying to lead us away from what enslaves us to what will bring us eternal happiness. This always involves forsaking our ways for God's ways. As with the Exodus, this journey takes time, will probably involve mistakes on our part, and requires that we be willing to trust God. If we do, God will always be faithful to his promises. As with many stories in the Bible,

---

185 Song of Solomon
186 Isaiah: 62:5
187 Hosea
188 Isaiah, 49:15
189 Exodus, 12:25
190 MT 13:3-9

the Exodus story is timeless because it describes truths that are independent of time.

This God of love who makes promises is also a God of justice. When those he has made promises to fail to do their part, there are always consequences. Whether it be Adam and Eve leaving the garden, the Israelite people being exiled by the Babylonians, or Judas taking his own life, there are always consequences.

Some interpret these consequences as an indication that God is a harsh judge. Scripture demonstrates otherwise. God asks those who think him harsh to consider whether their troubles are God's doing or of their own making.[191] In most cases, the most severe punishment God renders is to step back and let the offender do exactly what he or she pleases. And then be forced to live with the inevitable consequences. Think of Judas. Besides, God is always ready to forgive and forget. Think of Peter after his betrayal, and Paul after persecuting those who believed in Jesus.

The prodigal son parable, another story of timeless truth (and obviously one of my favorites), is particularly helpful when we try to understand God's justice. When the younger son demands his inheritance, the father does not discipline him for his unacceptable behavior. He gives him exactly what he asks for. After the son leaves, the father's sole desire is for his son to return. He spends each day watching and waiting in sadness. Meanwhile, the son gets himself into all kinds of trouble. These troubles are the consequences of decisions he has made. Finally, the son decides to return to his father because he is starving. The father spots him when he is still a long way off and runs to meet him. The son starts to tell his father what he thinks his father wants to hear. The father, overjoyed his son has returned, refuses to listen and instead calls for a great celebration.

What a wonderful form of justice!

The Bible helps us realize God is also a God of the unexpected. His thoughts are not our thoughts and his ways are not our ways.[192]

In his interactions with humankind, God always seems to confound and surprise. When God decided to enter human history to reveal his love, why didn't he pick a well-established nation? Why did he prefer to start communicating with a rag-tag group of twelve wandering tribes? In a culture that places the greatest responsibilities on the firstborn, why did God always seek out the youngest son, as was the case with Jacob's son Joseph, or David. Why did God choose

191   Ezekiel 18:25
192   Isaiah 55:8

a young girl in the backwater town of Nazareth to be the mother of his Son? Why was his Son born in a stable? Why were shepherds from the lowest rung of society his first visitors? Why did Jesus ignore well-versed students of the law to choose twelve ordinary men as his first disciples? Why did Jesus choose to do the most menial labor imaginable—wash his disciples' feet—shortly before he died? I could go on and on; the examples are almost endless, but I think the point is clear. God seems to prefer the humble and less powerful for his most important work. He seems to use those willing to trust in him rather than recognized, self-possessed leaders. He seems to treat established power structures with disdain.

God also surprised by delivering on promises in ways beyond what seemed possible. God promised a Messiah. He never mentioned it would be his only Son. His angel told Mary her son would be important. The angel never mentioned she would be remembered as the Mother of God. The apostles were asked to leave everything to follow Jesus. They were never told they would become saints. Jesus said he would have to be killed before being raised from the dead. No one imagined he would literally return to them from the dead, the first sign of God's promise that all who believe would live forever.

Indeed, God's ways are not our ways.

I find this idea intoxicating. For it means that God's most important revelations come not from established authority but from the humble who are willing to love. It means the future of the Church, Christ's body on this earth, depends not so much on who is Pope or bishop but on how willing the People of God are to respond to God's promises. At a more personal level, it means I don't have to waste time worrying about how God will deal with my various concerns and crises. For I know that if I do my part, he will do his, most likely in a way that will surprise me and, over time, turn out better than I had thought possible.

The Bible gives us insights into the nature of God. It also gives us insights into our nature. The insights are not particularly flattering.

Scripture tells us God created us in his own image AND with the ability to live in paradise, so long as we promise to live by his rules. To say it another way, we find happiness by accepting that God is the source of all that leads us there.

Scripture also tells us the first chance we had, in the form of Adam and Eve, we reneged on our part of the deal. We have been doing the same ever since, making choices premised on the assumption we can achieve complete happiness on our own, that we can create our own gods. That love is getting our way. If God is a promise maker, we are promise breakers.

The pattern revealed in the Bible goes as follows: God offers his love, we promise to live in his way, we decide we know better, we get in trouble, we suffer, God forgives, God offers his love, etc. The Exodus story of the journey through the desert to the Promised Land is a wonderful example of this pattern. The people quickly forget what God has done for them and begin second-guessing Moses. Soon they are challenging God's wisdom. The trip is too long, the way too difficult. They even experiment with false gods, getting themselves into all kinds of trouble. However, God always gives them another opportunity to be faithful, and eventually they get to their destination.

Once they reach the Promised Land, the pattern continues. The people prosper and eventually decide they need a king. When God points out they already have him, the people insist they need an earthly king so they can be like other nations. Reluctantly God agrees. A nation-state is born with David as reigning monarch. Jerusalem is founded, the city dedicated in love to God. David's son Solomon succeeds him. Solomon prays only for wisdom and is rewarded by God with abundance. The Jewish nation reaches its pinnacle of affluence. But then Solomon decides he can make room for other gods in HIS kingdom. Before long, the Jewish nation splits in two, and the long period of decline ensues, ending eventually in the exile of the people from their homeland.

The pattern is the same throughout the rest of The Old Testament. In fact, the prophets all speak about it. Unfortunately, the history of most Christian communities since then is eerily similar. The most discouraging thing about this pattern is that we never seem to learn. We are indeed stiff-necked people.

At the risk of sounding repetitive, the Bible stories that cover this pattern are timeless. At times we think the journey is too long or too difficult. We make the mistake of assuming we can control our own destiny. We fail to recognize the reality of the Divine in our lives. We even get used to living an unfulfilling existence, assuming enduring joy and unconditional love are unattainable.

Fortunately, Scripture reveals another side to our nature: the ability to recognize and return God's love, trusting in his goodness. To be faithful. The stories of Abraham, the Patriarchs, Moses, the Prophets, Mary, her husband Joseph, eleven of the twelve Apostles, and several of Jesus' female disciples, among others, all make this point.

The unusual story of Job describes the faithful response to God's love in a unique way. Job is devoted to God. He also leads a happy, fulfilling life. The Devil confronts God with the assertion that Job is devoted to God only because he leads such a good life. He dares God to let him introduce misfortune into Job's life. God acquiesces. Job immediately begins to experience various misfortunes. Three friends accuse him of responsibility for his difficulties, asserting he has done something that is objectionable to God. Job disagrees. Even though he cannot understand or explain his difficulties, Job steadfastly trusts the goodness of God.

Undaunted, the Devil goes back to God and once again dares God to let him introduce even greater misfortune into Job's life. God, confident in Job's faith, acquiesces once again. Job loses everything, including all his possessions and even his family. He ends up with nothing but a terribly diseased body. His three friends are even more insistent that Job has caused his own downfall by some terrible wrongdoing. For his part, Job knows he has done nothing wrong, and he remains convinced God will vindicate him. So much so he decides to challenge God to a trial.

The ensuing encounter with God convinces Job once again of God's supremacy and ends with Job's humble submission to the will of God, whatever that will is. The Devil gives up, astounded at Job's willingness to trust in God's goodness in the face of overwhelming difficulty. God is pleased with his faithful servant, and the story ends with Job enjoying abundance in his life greater than he had ever imagined.

The culminating act in the love story called the Bible is God's decision to send his only Son into the world, not to condemn the world, but so the world might be saved through him. Jesus spoke with the voice of God and touched with the touch of God. He came to proclaim good news of his Father's Kingdom: God created us in his own image and with the ability to live in paradise, so long as we promise to live by his rules. Said another way, we find our eternal home by accepting that God is the source of all that leads us there.

Jesus taught the Kingdom of God's love is available to all who are willing to love God and one another in return. He preached this love is more powerful than evil, our indifference, even the power of death. Jesus the Christ was the model of faithfulness to the end, sacrificing himself on our behalf to institute a new covenant based on forgiveness.

I have benefited from studying all parts of the Bible, but I always find myself drawn most powerfully to the four Gospels. They represent four views of Jesus. As such they present a more complete image than only one account would. A good analogy would be a 3D image. It appears slightly out of focus until the proper glasses are used. Once the glasses are in place, the image is more realistic, with a greater sense of perspective. In the case of the Gospels, our "glasses" are faith (openness to the power of the Divine) combined with a basic understanding of the communities for which the four Gospels were written.

For those of you who would like to take greater advantage of the great gift called the Bible or Holy Scripture, I suggest the following:

1. Read Matthew 16:13–16; this is the reason for Holy Scripture, to help you answer the question "Who do you say that I am?"[193]

2. Read the Gospels, in the order in which they were written (Mark, Matthew, Luke, and John).

3. Study with others; reflect/pray on Scripture by yourself. When studying with others, you can ask someone with training to lead your group, or you can use one of the many good outlines available for self-study groups, or you can just meet and discuss what specific preselected passages mean to each of you. In all cases, find a way to understand the four communities for which the Gospels were written.

4. Remember, this is Good News. If it does not seem like good news to you, assume you do not understand it. Seek the good news.

5. Finally, always try to apply the passages you are studying to your life today. One of the characteristics of divinely inspired material is that it is timeless. It can give different insights to different people at different times. It can also provide changing guidance to the same person over time.

To help you gain a better understanding of these suggestions, particularly the last two, I would like to conclude our discussion of

193   MT 16:15

Scripture with three examples of my own personal meditation on specific Gospel passages. As with other parts of this book, each is preceded by a reference to a Gospel passage that should be read first (have you noticed how much easier it has become?).

Life's Storms: *Matthew 14:22–33*

One of the many things Biblical scholars like to debate is whether any of Jesus' "nature miracles" actually happened. When I say "nature miracles" I am referring to miracles where Jesus changed the course of nature, as in the calming of the storm in this Gospel. Such miracles are grouped together to differentiate them from Jesus' healing miracles, the veracity of which is questioned by almost no one.

I am sure those who debate this subject feel they are doing something useful. It seems like a waste of time to me. You see, I know these miracles happened, because they still happen. They have happened to me. From time to time, there are storms in my life. When they occur, I have a tendency to wonder why Jesus didn't prevent them. Or at least help me avoid them. Sometimes I even wonder whether he knows I exist, whether he exists. Often, I can taste the fear, the anxiety. Yes, I know these things; they have been part of my life.

I also know that when I am willing to overcome my fear to trust in the goodness of God, I experience a sense of great calm in my life. Let me give you an example.

As you know, I have cancer. The first time I was faced with this reality, I was completely disoriented. I felt alone, even abandoned. I was filled with fear. Gradually, though, I was able to accept I had a choice. I could either live with fear as my master or I could choose to trust in the reality of a God who is always with me, gently leading me. Almost magically, the fear would dissipate, a sense of calm taking its place.

I think it is no accident that all stories of Jesus calming stormy waters include the statements "Be not afraid" and "You of little faith." Faith is the willingness to open ourselves to the power of God's love, the willingness to trust; fear is the opposite of faith, for it shuts us down, leaving us mired in a universe of one.

So why did Matthew's Gospel add the vignette of Peter's attempt to walk on water? My answer is simple: because we all have the power to do so, to traverse stormy waters in freedom and a sense of peace, until we let fear return. How do I know this to be true? Every time I have learned my cancer has taken a turn for the worse, I feel myself beginning to sink. I guess I just can't help it. And there I am with Peter, saying, "Lord, save me!'

And he always has.

And that's the good news.

When I Get Discouraged: *Matthew 14:13–21*

Sometimes I get discouraged. Life seems gray and almost pointless. I want to go off by myself, away from everyone, and just be...well, just be.

This usually happens when I get tired, I've got too much to do, my wife needs what seems at the moment to be an unreasonable amount of help, or I have just failed in an attempt to help someone. Maybe it's my pride. But I think it's feeling that what I do doesn't matter. Now, don't tell me; I know. I preach that it's the effort that counts, not the result, but sometimes that's hard, particularly when someone you care for is suffering and destined to suffer even more.

Sometimes I get discouraged.

Maybe you have gone through the same kind of thing. I know Jesus did. And reading about his experience makes me feel better. It probably happened many times, but I particularly like the story in Matthew about how Jesus dealt with the death of his cousin John.

At first, he did just what I would do. He wanted to get away. We don't know what Jesus was feeling as he stepped into a boat and left his followers, but I'd guess it wasn't pleasant. John was not only a relative but had been instrumental in helping Jesus begin his own ministry. Besides, he was killed for doing something very similar to what Jesus was doing.

We don't know how Jesus felt. What we do know is that life just wouldn't leave him alone. Soon there were people looking for him, clamoring for his help. Thousands, we are told. So what did Jesus do? He came ashore, cured their sick, and then that evening, when it became apparent they didn't have enough to eat, performed a miracle to feed them all.

Whenever I read this story, I feel better. Reenergized. Because in it, Jesus reminds me that when life just won't leave me alone—and that's often—there's something I can do. Jesus reminds me that when I am willing to be "moved with pity," to be compassionate, I can get out of myself and back into focusing on the needs of others. And most importantly I think, Jesus reminds me that what might look like failure to me, nothing but a measly five loaves and two fish, might be just what he needs to do marvelous things.

And that's the good news.

Who Do You Say That I Am? *Matthew 16:13–16*

One day, Jesus asked his disciples two questions: "Who do people say that I am?" and "Who do *you* say that I am?" This second question must have been very important. When Peter responded with "You are the Christ, the son of the living God," Jesus talked about the formation of his church for the only time in all the Gospels. What made this second question so special?

Someone else introduces all of us to the idea of Jesus. For most of us this was one parent or both parents. Then we learned more from other people, primarily in our religious education classes. As we matured we learned still more from our priest during Sunday Mass. I doubt any of us would have a problem answering the first question. Neither did Jesus' disciples.

The problem arises when we try to answer the second question. Most of us don't have an answer because we have never thought about the question. As a result, we almost always answer the first question again, never realizing we have made a mistake, never focusing on the question so important to Jesus.

During his ministry, Jesus called people to decide for themselves what was and what was not important to them. He told stories, called parables, which required thinking to discern the lesson he was trying to teach. For the most part, he would not answer questions. He would reply with a question of his own or a story so his listener would—you've got it—have to think. The only time he consistently answered questions was in his arguments with religious leaders. One of his criticisms of this group? Their unwillingness to think for themselves about who Jesus was.

Most people Jesus encountered were waiting for the government, their religious leaders, or their neighbors to make their lives better. It seems little has changed in this regard. Jesus' message was and still is simple. Waiting for others to make your life better is a fool's errand. Only when you think through what's important to you, and then decide to change, will the world around you begin to improve. And this kind of personal change is so much easier when you know who Jesus is.

It's that simple.

And that's the good news.

Summary

God has given each of us free gifts, which, when accepted and used, will help us live life more fully. They are free gifts because we have done nothing to deserve them and because there are no strings attached. These gifts must simply be accepted and opened.

It is my hope the seven gifts covered in this book will prompt you to think of others that have helped you.

Home

Home is not a geographic place. It is any family environment where I know I am accepted and loved just I am, where I am able to forgive completely because I know I have been forgiven, my mistakes are merely lessons learned, and everything belongs. Role models, usually found in families, help me form life principles that can lead me home. My Parish is one kind of home. God has prepared an eternal home available to every one of us.

Mary as role model

Mary is an extraordinary role model in learning how to deal with the Divine. She was willing to devote her life to doing God's will, trusting completely in his goodness. She is a model of faithfulness.

Divine mercy

Jesus came to remind us God's mercy is infinite and available to anyone willing to seek it, trust in it, and become God's mercy to others. We become God's mercy to others when we enter another's chaos, on their terms, our only goal being their well-being.

Real Presence

Jesus the Christ is truly present, body and blood, soul and divinity, in the Sacrament of the Eucharist. Believe and you will see.

Reconciliation

We all sin. At times we all fail to love as Jesus taught us to love. Sin makes us less because it weakens or destroys our relationships. Only God can forgive sin. Reconciliation is the Sacrament in which God forgives our sins and helps restore our relationships.

Body of Christ

We become active members of the Body of Christ when we, as baptized Christians, allow ourselves to be transformed by the Holy

Spirit so we can live and work together as one, holy, catholic, and apostolic family.

Scripture

Holy Scripture, or the Bible, is the divinely inspired love story about God's effort to lead us home and our reaction to his overtures. Scripture helps us understand the nature of God and our nature, providing timeless insights into how to experience more joy in our lives.

VI
Choices

In Brief

Some of God's gifts require more determined effort on our part to realize their benefits. Please don't get discouraged by this statement; I am not trying to sound like a strict diet or strenuous exercise advocate. Everything covered involves something we tend to do anyway, or are capable of doing by simply deciding it's important enough to do. Hence the title "Choices."

There is pretty good evidence that if you do the same thing for thirty days, such as eating breakfast before your first cup of coffee, that action, whatever it is, will become a habit. You will then be predisposed to continue doing the same thing every day. Sort of like a law of physics: things in motion tend to stay in motion. Used correctly, this trait is itself a great gift, for it gives us the ability to change the way we view and live life, one habit at a time.

Each of the choices we will examine can easily become a habit if consciously repeated for relatively short periods of time. I know this from my own life as well as the lives of those I have known. In the same way I also know that each of these choices can help us live life more fully, and that ignoring these choices has just the opposite effect. Because all choices, even the choice to do nothing, have consequences.

As you read the following pages, please do not try to implement everything at one time. Pick one or two, and then focus on them until you are comfortable with the results they produce in your life. Then, before you start taking those benefits for granted, select another one or two. Remember: God wants you to lead a fuller and more complete life. It is his will. You have a pretty powerful supporting cast!

Finally, this list is not meant to be inclusive. As I have already mentioned, the spiritual journey has no end. It just keeps getting better. As such, you and I can both discover more choices along the way. Perhaps you know some of them already, if you just give it some thought. In this way, as in some many others, God is good.

Attitudes

Matthew 5:1–12

Very early in life, we each develop a structured way of seeing the world around us. We do so to help us interpret the seemingly random nature of life. Think of this process as constructing a set of glasses that brings life into focus. Interestingly, we each develop our own unique set of glasses, which helps explain why people react differently when confronted by the same experience. When unexpectedly encountering a homeless man, one person may feel compassion, another fear, still another disdain. These reactions are different because three people literally see the same person differently.

These "life" glasses are extremely important to our well-being. In large measure they determine whether we are adventuresome or timid, optimistic or pessimistic, hopeful or hopeless. They strongly influence our image of self, others, and our God. Unfortunately, no one has the perfect set of glasses. So the important question is how do we go about improving them?

When an event occurs in our lives, the way we view that event through our set of glasses determines our initial reaction. We call these reactions feelings or emotions, which in and of themselves are neither good nor bad because we have no conscious control over them. They simply are.

It would be easy to underestimate the importance of our feelings. More than any other single factor, they represent who we are. My feelings are not your feelings, and your feelings are not my feelings. I am the only one who causes and experiences my feelings. To say or think that someone or something else does is a form of self-delusion. Because our glasses are unique, so are our feelings. One of the great mistakes we all make is to assume others will react the same way we will to any specific circumstance. Our feelings may be similar, but they are always unique. Just as we are unique.

There is no true friendship, or, more importantly, true love, without sharing how we feel. This tends to run counter to a culture that thrives on meaningless conversation and superficial happiness. The truth is that if I am going to love I must be willing to share who I am, without condition. I must tell you my feelings.[194] My true feelings, including my fears, my insecurities, my dislikes. There is no real communication, the lifeblood of all meaningful relationships,

---

194 *Seasons of the Heart,* John Powell SJ, p. 164

without the communication of feelings. Remember, feelings are neither good nor bad, they just are. Finally, if I choose to hide or bury feelings, they will not stay hidden. They will merely reappear in less attractive ways, much to the detriment of healthy relationships and even my emotional well-being.

When an event occurs in our lives, we feel an emotion based on how we perceive that event. We have no direct control over this reaction. Then the crucial moment occurs when we are capable of making a conscious decision about how to deal with this event. Another driver abruptly cuts in front of me without signaling. I perceive danger and feel anger. I pause for a moment but then decide I am justified in being angry at the driver's thoughtless actions, and start fantasizing about how I might get even. Or, as the same event occurs, I pause for a moment and decide I shouldn't let the thoughtless actions of another disturb my day. In either case I am choosing an attitude.

Attitudes are similar to feelings but differ in several ways. For our purposes, the most important is that we can consciously change our attitudes, despite how we feel, independent of (although influenced by) our "glasses." We can choose an attitude by just deciding to do so. Then, if our choice has been a good one, we will experience the benefits of that choice, which reinforces the tendency to choose that particular attitude (obviously, the reverse is also true). In the example I used in the last paragraph, a choice of continued anger tends to have lasting negative effects, sometimes for hours, even a whole day. Have you ever had what you perceived as a negative experience that then seemed to ruin your whole day? I know I have, and I am embarrassed to admit that it is often the simplest of things, like discovering I gained an unexpected pound when I do my weekly weigh-in.

On the other hand, the person who is cut off by another driver, and decides to not let the thoughtless actions of another disturb his day, is freed from harmful anger and is able to take full advantage of the day. Our experiences reinforce the decisions we make regarding our attitudes.

All attitudes have consequences, and the primary consequence is the effect on the one holding the attitude. Attitudes like guilt, remorse, and anger constrict my view of reality, reducing my ability to grow and experience life more fully. Think of it as a darkening of my glasses. Hypocrisy, the conscious decision to pretend my view of reality is different than it actually is, is a particularly damaging attitude. It is pretending I can see perfectly when I am actually blind.

Positive attitudes like honesty with self, acceptance of others' frailties, and forgiveness help me grow in my willingness to trust and my ability to see more clearly the goodness in life. Positive attitudes are the way we change our view of reality. They enhance our glasses, which means that over time, they are the way we improve our initial emotional reactions to the events in our lives. In a very real way, we become who we choose to be.

Attitudes are the way we become more, or less. Our attitudes are the only thing in life we control completely. Think of them as God's gift to us, the key to his Kingdom.

"Follow me" is the invitation Jesus issues to each one of us. This invitation may sound inviting or foreboding, depending on our point of view, but in all cases it soon becomes clear that he is asking us to leave our old life behind to travel to wherever he wants to lead us. Where is this?

If I had to recommend one Scripture passage to answer this question, it would be Matthew's rendition of the Beatitudes. When Jesus first taught them, whether at one time on a mountainside or, as some think, throughout his public ministry, they represented the core of what he asked of his followers.

Clearly, Jesus was espousing a preferential option for the poor. But he was also doing so much more. Unfortunately, it is relatively easy to miss the primary point of the Beatitudes because Jesus was using a prophetic formula unfamiliar to most of us. But once this prophetic formula is understood, the message is both clear and exhilarating.

The formula contains four key words or phrases. The first is the word "Blessed." All eight Beatitudes start with this word. "Blessed" means happiness: complete, unalterable, fulfilling happiness. Think of joy. In fact, the word "beatitude" literally means blessedness, bliss, supreme happiness.[195] Jesus calls us to leave our old life behind so he can lead us to fulfillment. Life lived fully, in preparation for life lived perfectly in union with his Father.

The Beatitudes respond to the natural desire for happiness. This desire is of divine origin. God has placed it in the human heart in order to draw people to the One who alone can fulfill it.[196]

---

195 New Oxford Dictionary
196 Catechism, 1718

The next key word is what we translate as the word "will." Think of it more like the word "shall," which not only connotes the future but also is emphatic in its certainty. This happiness is guaranteed. Two of the Beatitudes use the word "is" instead of "will." In these two cases, happiness is already available if we choose to recognize it.

The next word or phrase (e.g. poor in spirit, mourn, meek, hunger, and thirst) represents an attitude. Jesus did NOT endorse poverty, sadness, hunger, and thirst as ways of life. He did teach that our attitudes are the keys to his Kingdom. This should be reassuring because, as already mentioned, our attitudes are the only thing in life we control completely, and as we change our attitudes, the way we perceive the world around us changes.

Specifically, Jesus taught that humility (poor of spirit), compassion (mourn and meek), forgiveness (merciful and peacemakers), and a willingness to trust in the goodness of God by striving to do his will (righteousness, even when insulted or persecuted, and pure of heart) are the attitudes fundamental to living life as his follower.

In my opinion, Christian humility is the fundamental attitude we who call ourselves followers of Jesus should seek. Christian humility recognizes our dependence on God: he is the Creator and Provider of life; he is the path to beatitude; we are the created.

At the same time, Christian humility recognizes we have been created in goodness as a unique expression of God. It is good to be me, an attitude that, in and of itself, is life-changing *if fully embraced*. Of course, as we accept that it is good to be who we are, just as we are, we must also acknowledge we are imperfect. We are fractions in the process of becoming whole numbers[197]. As such, mistakes happen. Viewed properly, they are merely indications we are not yet done growing. They are lessons learned. Finally, Christian humility requires that we accept others as also being created in goodness, as unique expressions of God, also capable of both good and the more problematic.

Some believe there is really only one Beatitude: Blessed are the poor in spirit. The remaining seven just help explain the first. I think there is real merit in this idea, because as we strive to be more humble we become more like Jesus himself (I am gentle and humble of heart[198]). Besides, the first Beatitude is one of only two using the verb "is." The benefits of humility are available immediately.

---

197 *Seasons of the Heart,* John Powell S.J.
198 MT 11:29

Compassion, in its simplest form, means the willingness to enter into the feelings of another. When one is willing to be compassionate, it is so much easier to express our true feelings (mourn) and be gentle with others (meek) because we experience their pain or joy, or just their point of view. We experience their uniqueness.

We have already mentioned the life-giving effects of forgiveness, and that it has two parts: the act of forgiving (willingness to show mercy) and the effort to be reconciled (peacemakers).

Finally, there are the three Beatitudes that deal with seeking and doing the will of God. The notion of "pure of heart" has often been limited to sexual purity. Clearly, God does not condone abuses of his great gift of sexuality. But the intent of the Beatitude is much broader. "Pure of heart" means to seek the will of God in all things. To be pure (vs. immoral or flawed) in our efforts to follow God's will for us.

Righteousness, the subject of two other Beatitudes, is often confused with the idea of self-righteousness. The difference lies in our point of reference. The righteous person tries to do what he or she feels God would have him do, and wants to do the right thing by God's standards. The self-righteous person is focused on self: what I think is right is right.

Pure of heart and righteousness both mean attempting to live in accordance with God's will. Which, if you think about it, brings us back to Christian humility.

These four attitudes have great power to change us, and those with whom we come in contact, for the better. Yesterday, as I was driving to my daily exercise and half listening to NPR, I heard the word "compassion" being used. The show host was interviewing two inmates from Louisiana's Angola prison. This prison has been known as the most violent prison in the United Sates, used exclusively for lifers—inmates with no chance of parole.

In 1997, long-time warden Burl Cain decided to institute a hospice program for dying inmates. The two inmates being interviewed were hospice volunteers. Both were sharing the changes they had experienced in their own lives once they started making an effort to be present to another human being. They started with the fact no one wants to be alone, particularly when death is approaching. They shared the perspective this experience had given them, from sorrow (often for the first time) over the crimes they had committed to their desire to help others lead more meaningful lives. They talked about how the changes they had made in their lives had helped other inmates (outside the hospice environment) change theirs. I think they used the word "compassion" seven or eight times.

The violent crime rate at Angola prison has decreased seventy-five percent since the formation of the Angola prison hospice program.

These four attitudes or virtues (what is a virtue other than an attitude become habit?) have great power. I think this is true because they constitute what I like to refer to as the "Love Attitude." Obviously, no one can use all four or even one of these attitudes perfectly. But remember, we are beings in the process of becoming more. This is a journey. We must only be willing. And then make the effort.

If I may, let me add a word of practical advice. Humility, compassion, forgiveness, and righteousness (doing the right thing) usually appear as much smaller, more practical shifts in attitudes. For example, the driver who chooses to remain angry in our previous example could either be unwilling to forgive, or just willing to let anger ruin his or her day. The driver who decides to let go of that initial irritation may do so out of a desire to forgive or, more likely, a willingness to be compassionate (maybe the other driver is having a bad day) or, most likely, a simple inclination to do the right thing (why should I let someone else ruin my day?).

God has given us a way to help us evaluate the decisions we make regarding our attitudes. Remember moral conscience? One way our conscience helps us is in the way it encourages love attitudes. At the end of your day, or after a particularly difficult encounter, review how you dealt with the day or specific encounter. How did your attitudes make you feel afterward? If you felt discouraged, empty, frustrated, or even a little embarrassed, it is highly likely the attitudes you chose were not forms of humility, compassion, forgiveness, or righteousness. If, on the other hand, you feel better about yourself, or sense you did the right thing, or are even pleased with the outcome, you are on the right track. Trust me—if you are willing to reflect on your choices, they will get better. Perhaps it won't occur to you, but if it does, you can even thank the Holy Spirit for his help.

A related exercise involves identifying and reflecting on the feelings that preceded a particular attitude. This is especially true when the feelings were negative, like shame or fear. Very often, examining the causes (always internal) of a particular feeling can lead to a more positive attitude toward others or ourselves. New positive attitudes then slowly change the way we view reality, eventually improving our emotional responses.

Remember my mention of life principles in our discussion of the gift called "Home?" I mentioned that Jesus lived with one overriding life principle, the principle to love. In my opinion, the four attitudes we have discussed, if practiced, will foster the growth of your own love principle. Like the merchant who finds a priceless pearl and sells everything he has to own it,[199] you will know you have discovered a gift of incalculable value.

Finally, the last word or phrase in each Beatitude describes a characteristic of God's Kingdom: comforted, inheriting the land, being satisfied, being shown mercy, seeing God, and knowing we are truly children of God. All these phrases are meant to be descriptions of God's Kingdom from Holy Scripture. This is where Jesus wants to lead us: to his Father's Kingdom, where we know joy complete (beatitude), because we are home.

There is much more to learn about and from the Beatitudes and the teachings that follow in Matthew's Gospel, but the fundamental idea is one we should rejoice over and never lose sight of: Jesus calls us to live life fully in this world in preparation for living life perfectly in the next: perfect happiness, joy, and fulfillment, in union with God, forever. For those who choose to respond positively to Jesus' invitation to follow him, it is a journey beyond our ability to even imagine.

Blessed are we who are willing to believe, for the Kingdom of God is ours.

---

199   MT 13: 45-46

Seeing

Luke 23:39–43

I began the last chapter by saying we each develop a structured way of seeing the world around us early in life. This in good part is caused by our desire to bring a sense of order to the seemingly random nature of life. But it also has something to do with the way we learn.

As soon as we enter formal classes, we are taught to learn by comparing. We learn what something is by learning what it is not. An apple is an apple because it is not an orange. Blue is blue because it is not red. I am male and you are female because we are different.

This beginning is then expanded to include an emphasis on believing what can be proved with logical reasoning. We test whatever we would like to believe (our hypothesis) with some form of rigorous test or tests, all to prove something is *either* true *or* not true. Thomas used this approach when he said he would not believe Jesus had been raised from the dead until he could see and touch him. We are taught to think like Thomas.

At the heart of all this are three fundamental rules of logic, which have been with us since ancient Greece:

> *A is A*, or the law of identity (an apple is an apple)
> *A is not B*, or the law of contradiction (an apple is not an orange)
> *A and B are never the same*, or the law of the excluded third (an apple can never be an apple and an orange at the same time)[200]

For our purposes, let us call this approach "either/or" thinking.

In case you are wondering, I am not trying to say this approach is bad or wrong. Education would not be education without it. It enables productive abstract thinking about almost any subject. Almost all technological advances in our society have been based on it. We would have a hard time living the lives we now live without "either/or" thinking. What I am saying is this: "either/or" thinking is necessary, but it is not sufficient.

Unfortunately, "either/or" thinking often leads to all-or-nothing conclusions. We are good; they are bad. We win; they lose. All-or-nothing thinking quickly merges with exclusionary thinking. In

---

200   *A New Way of Seeing*, Richard Rohr

almost all cases, what we understand least is excluded. "My school, team, religion is the best for me" evolves into "My school, team, religion is the best" to "My school, team, religion is the only real school, team, or religion." If we are right, then you must be wrong. You don't belong. Major "isms" like nationalism, racism, clericalism, fascism, and sexism are all built on this premise. The current malaise in the United States political system also reflects this tendency. In every case, whatever is excluded is what is not well understood. We fear the unknown, treating it as less desirable than what we are more familiar with.

Exclusionary thinking is a small half step away from "better than/less than" judgments. For centuries, the Roman Catholic Church taught it was the only true Church. Some Roman Catholic priests still do, despite clear statements to the contrary by Church leadership (covered in *There Are Many Paths*). "Only true" Church meant that all other Churches were not true and therefore somehow less and inferior faith traditions. Thomas Jefferson, author of the Declaration of Independence ("We hold these truths to be self-evident, that all men are created equal...."), also owned slaves because he felt they were inferior. A rabid Rex Sox baseball fan loves his team and hates the Yankees. At times, we all tend to think in all-or-nothing terms, excluding groups or ideas or even foods we are less familiar with as inferior. We tend to see what we have been taught to see. "Either/or" thinking alters the "life glasses" we use to see life.

At the heart of these shortcomings is a simple reality. The more we learn about God's creation (with the benefit of logical thinking), the more we realize everything in life is connected. Life is not "either/or." All of God's creation and our experience within it are "both/and." I am a unique creation. At the same time I am part of a larger universe. I literally cannot exist without the larger universe.

At a more personal level, I am not always good. I am not always right. I am clearly not a saint. But I am also not just the reverse. I am a mixture of both: good and bad, right and wrong, saint and sinner. So are you. So are we all. A is not always A (I am not always good); B is not always B (I am not always bad); sometimes A and B (like good and bad) exist at the same time. And free will gives us the opportunity to become more, in either direction.

All of which brings us to the subject of mystery (that which we can know without ever fully understanding). There is no way to logically explain the great mysteries (love, great suffering, death,

God, and eternity.[201]) The longer I study human behavior, the more convinced I am that at times we are all mysteries.

Mysteries connect us in ways that go far beyond biological or environmental connections. Mysteries are not to be feared or treated with disdain, for they lie at the heart of learning to live with joy.

One of the arguments often used in Roman Catholic theological debate is the threat of being labeled a relativist, meaning that you think knowledge, truth, and morality exist in relation to culture, society, or historical context and are not absolute.[202] In a more practical context, a relativist is a wishy-washy stand-for-nothing compromiser. It would be easy for some to misinterpret "both/and" thinking, or our inability to fully understand mysteries, as relativism. You mean there is no absolute good, no absolute evil? You mean I shouldn't strive to be perfect? And so on.

I believe in absolute good (God), the reality of evil, and the effects of both loving and sinful behavior. I also believe in seeking the truth. And the truth is that when we complement "either/or" thinking for problem solving with "both/and" thinking for living, we are able to see and live life in a more robust way.

It seems the Roman Catholic Church agrees. Almost all of our most important Traditions require "both/and" thinking. Several examples might help to demonstrate this fact.

The Father, Son and Holy Spirit are each *both* unique *and* yet part of one. The Son is the Son (A is A). The Son is not the Father (A is not B). The Father and the Son are one (oops).

Jesus is *both* true God *and* true man.

Mary is *both* true virgin *and* true mother.

The Eucharist is *both* bread and wine *and* the body and blood of Jesus.

Jesus' life and teachings are also filled with examples of "both/and" thinking.

He came *both* to proclaim the good news *and to* die for our sins.

He taught his Father's love was like the sun. It rises on *both* the good *and* the evil.[203]

His Kingdom is *both* here *and* coming.[204]

---

201   *A New Way of Seeing,* Richard Rohr
202   *New Oxford Dictionary*
203   MT 5:45
204   MK 1:15, LK 10:11, LK 17:21, LK 21:29-31, MK 13:32

The first will be *both* first (now) *and* last (later). The last shall be first.[205]

The exalted will be humbled; the humble exalted.[206]

Those who lose their life...will save it.[207]

Give *both* to Caesar the things that are Caesar's *and* to God the things that are God's.[208]

As Jesus was dying on the cross, a condemned criminal asked Jesus to remember him in his Kingdom. Jesus replied, "Truly I tell you, today you will be with me in Paradise."[209] That condemned criminal was *both* sinner *and* saint.

The Roman Catholic Church clearly recognizes the importance of "both/and" thinking. The head of our Church, Jesus Christ, used "both/and" thinking in an inspired way. Both should help us open ourselves more fully to the reality of our lived experience, where:

- Everything is connected.
- All humans (including us) can be both good and, at times, not so good.
- That which we do not yet fully understand is not to be feared.
- Mystery is the source of our most important treasures.

Opening ourselves in these ways helps us see more clearly. It also helps us realize mistakes are mere lessons learned, and eventually that everything truly does belong.

Making a conscious attempt (as in attitude) to use "both/and" thinking has several practical benefits.

Most of us struggle with our sense of self-worth. Part of the reason for this unfortunate reality is "either/or" thinking. I am either good or bad. Lovable or unlovable. Others appear to be either good or bad, but I know I am neither, or both. Accepting we are a mixture of the good and the more problematic helps us realize we are indeed beings in process. Humility becomes more natural. We are not yet done, and what is most important is not so much where we are at the moment but the direction in which we are headed (in the end, everything is spiritual). It is good to be me. Say that a couple of

---

205   MT 19:30
206   LK 14:11
207   LK 17:33
208   MK 12:17
209   LK 23:43

times, remembering that what you consider to be your imperfections may just be a good part of what others love about you.

A more positive attitude toward self inevitably alters our attitudes toward others. Seeing what connects us rather than what separates us makes it easier to feel compassion and be willing to forgive.

> We compare less, identify with more,
> Judging less, accepting more,
> Condemning less, praising more,
> Less exclusive, more inclusive,
> Righteous in the eyes of our Father,
> Divine mercy to others,
> the living Body of Christ.

Healing

Luke 7:11–17

Jesus was willing to reach out to anyone he met who needed healing. While careful to avoid those who merely wanted a display of his power (Lord, we want to see a sign from you[210]), he always healed those who were sincerely seeking help. He never refused anyone. Even people he had been taught by his religion to avoid: the Canaanite woman and her daughter in Matthew's Gospel,[211] the Samaritan woman at Jacob's well in John's Gospel.[212] Jesus' healing miracles were a mainstay of his public ministry. They were the most common and most dramatic way he demonstrated the Kingdom was becoming a reality.

A closer look at these healing miracles reveals a specific pattern in many of them. Luke's story of Jesus' miracle in the village of Nain provides a useful case study to help us understand these common traits.

As they enter the town, Jesus and his followers encounter a funeral procession for the only son of a widow. The woman no longer has any male family member, which is significant because such women are no longer considered part of the community. When Jesus sees the woman, he feels compassion for her. He cares. He says to her, "Do not weep" and, moving to the funeral bier carrying the dead son, touches it, saying, "Young, man, I say to you, rise." The boy sits up, and Jesus gives him back to his mother. Understandably, everyone is filled with awe and praises God.[213]

The three common elements are these:

1. Jesus feels compassion; he is willing to care.
2. He reaches out and touches, even though there is risk in doing so. In first- century Israel, it was commonly believed that any contact with a diseased, deformed, or dead person carried with it a significant risk. You might be stricken with the same evil spirit.
3. Finally, when successful in healing someone, Jesus did not ask for anything in return. His only goal was to help

---

210 MT 12:38, MT 16:1, MK 8:11, LK 11:16
211 MT 15:21-28
212 JN 4:1-42
213 LK 7:11-17

the affected person return to community, to relationship with loved ones.

These three traits are present in the majority of Jesus' healing miracles. If they sound vaguely familiar, it's because they are the components of what we have already defined as Divine Mercy (the willingness to enter the chaos of others, on their terms, with their well-being as the only goal).

When one or more of these elements are not present in a healing miracle, it is usually because the one missing is implied (the most common being specific mention of Jesus' compassion[214]) or the miracle is being used to teach a specific lesson. Examples include the importance of faith in the healing of the centurion's servant[215] and the daughter of the Canaanite woman,[216] and the importance of the love command in the Sabbath healings,[217] all of which violated the law for being done on the Sabbath, and all of which involved people with long-term disabilities.

There is one other point I would like to make using the Nain healing miracle. Jesus actually helped two people in this story. He cured the son, raising him from the dead. When I use the term "cure" I am referring to a change in the physical nature of the person affected. Jesus was able to cure people, giving sight to the blind, hearing to the deaf, speech to the mute, and life to the boy at Nain. Ever since, there have been people who have had this gift. But, for reasons only God knows, this gift is limited to a small number. We often refer to these people as healers, but technically speaking they are curers.

Jesus cured the boy and, by returning him to his mother (the one for whom he felt compassion), he healed his mother. Not only did she have her son back, but, because she once again had a male in her immediate family, she was able to return as an active member of her community. She was able to live life more fully.

Very few of us have been given the gift of curing. We have no choice in the matter. But we have all been given the gift of healing. We have all been given the capacity to care, to be compassionate. It is our choice. We have all been given the capability to reach out and

214   MK 8:22-26
215   MT 8:5-13
216   MT 15:22-28
217   MT 12:9-14, MK 3:1-6, LK 6:6-11, LK 13:10-17, LK 14:1-6, JN 5:1-10, JN 9:1-37

touch what hurts in another, even though it may involve risk. It is our choice. And when we have helped someone, we all have the freedom to seek nothing for ourselves, wanting instead only what is best for the one helped. Once again, it is our choice.

We, you and I, can be healers. You and I can work miracles. God's grace at work in the way God would have it used. Righteousness at its best. It is our choice.

The primary risk we face in trying to reach out and touch another is the same risk God faces when dealing with us: the risk of rejection. When Jesus was unable to perform miracles, it was because people rejected him.[218] We are not told how Jesus felt when this occurred, but we do know rejection is one of the most painful emotions we can experience. So the risk is real. This is why it is so important to remember we are responsible only for the effort, not the results. And when we are rebuffed by someone we are trying to help, "Shake the dust from your feet and leave. Yet be sure of this, the Kingdom of God is very near."[219]

Healing miracles can take all kinds of forms. The hopeless are able to recognize new beginnings because someone cares. The discouraged take heart because someone listens, really listens, to them. The depressed see new possibilities when they believe they are not alone on their journey. The terminally ill feel their first touch of everlasting peace as they feel the embrace of a loved one. The alcoholic sheds his addiction because other alcoholics help him through the difficult times.

Healing is real when we are willing to care, to risk touching another in an effort to help, and to ask for nothing in return. All signs of the Kingdom becoming a reality.

I have had the privilege of witnessing such miracles. Perhaps you have too. When I do, I am often struck by what may be the most important miracle: as we heal, so are we healed.

Which brings us to the subject of God's promises.

---

218   LK 4:16-30
219   LK 10:11-12

Promises

Matthew 7:7–11; Luke 6:37–38

God is a promise maker. Both the Old and the New Testaments contain examples of this phenomenon. God's promises are all variations of the great promise in the Exodus story. If we commit ourselves to be his people, making his ways our ways, he will lead us from whatever enslaves us to the Promised Land...the Kingdom...life lived with a greater sense of joy. It is The Journey Home. As such, all these promises represent gifts that require choices on our part.

The most basic choice is whether we want more from life, so much so that we are willing to change, breaking old habit patterns to form new ones.

Jesus came to proclaim the good news. The Kingdom was breaking in. But he spent very little time with those unwilling to change, the affluent, and religious leaders. He spent his time with sinners who were poor in spirit, those humble enough to know they were not yet complete. Those willing to trust in their God because they hungered and thirst for a better life.

Two of God's promises have had a particularly powerful effect on my life: Seek and you will find, and give and you will receive. You have read about them in the recommended Gospel passages. While I will limit myself to these two, please remember there are many more. Keep this in mind whenever you read or pray Scripture. You may be surprised by what you find that resonates in your own life.

Seek and you will find.

Perhaps only in retrospect is it apparent to me I have spent most of my life searching. For the longest time, I wasn't even sure what I was looking for. I have always been curious and willing to try new experiences, with the vague feeling I would someday discover something that would bring enduring happiness. Little did I know I was seeking. And because I did, incredible things appeared in my life. Several examples might help make the point.

I met and became friends with my future wife, Frannie, because I had gone to Boston after college to make my fortune. We met on a blind date. Her boyfriend had been sent to the Mediterranean by the Navy. I joined IBM because I was desperate for work to support my then-pregnant wife and happened to meet the local IBM branch manager, who had one more day before he lost authorization to hire a new salesman. I became a father, perhaps my greatest accomplishment, because I couldn't imagine life any other way.

When we began our time at St. Mary's in Ridgefield in the early 1970s, I started doing more in the Parish almost by accident. I continued because it made me feel better. I felt more whole. By 1978, I couldn't imagine my life without our Parish community. I also recognized the great gift of my wife and family, as well as the benefits of working for IBM. At times it seemed to me I was being too greedy to ask for more when I was already so blessed. But I was also learning a lot about prayer. So I started asking God to help me find his will for me. It seemed to me that if he really knew and cared more about me than I did about myself, he might have a better idea of what I needed. I was seeking.

Later that year, Father Charlie made the announcement about the permanent diaconate accepting candidates. I knew I had found something I had been seeking. As already mentioned, Frannie wasn't so sure.

Five years later, in 1983, one year after her Baptism, she asked if I was still interested in becoming a permanent deacon. When I told her I was, she consented to my applying. Four years later I was ordained. It was the same year I entered AA. The next year two of our daughters were married.

My wife, expanded family, diaconate ministry, and sobriety. What more could I want? I have learned the answer is more. Life could be even more meaningful. I was beginning to suspect the spiritual journey never ends. It just keeps getting better. I could feel the gratitude, but I wanted more. And so I have continued to seek. For a clearer understanding of God's will for me, for increased conscious contact with the Divine, for the grace always to be an example of his love.

Through this process, I gradually became aware of two realities. The first related to the passage "Ask, and it will be given to you; search and you will find; knock and the door will be opened. Everyone who asks, receives; everyone who searches finds; whoever knocks will have the door opened."[220] It occurred to me that God keeps his promises—in my life. Whenever I ask for what will help me live life more fully. Not necessarily on my schedule, rarely when I ask for a specific result, and never for anything related to material affluence.

---

220   MT 7:7-8

In first-century Israel, it was generally accepted that material affluence was a sign of God's blessing. Those with wealth were considered fortunate. As a result, Jesus' followers were astounded when he announced that such people were unlikely candidates for his Kingdom.

In the centuries since not much has changed. Affluence means influence, being one of the select. Our movies, advertising, even some of our more lavish churches celebrate wealth. Who wants to be a millionaire? Almost everyone, it seems. The unspoken premise is that material abundance, even excess, guarantees happiness. Unfortunately, lost in the rush to acquire more, bigger, and better is Jesus' teaching on the subject.

Jesus' basic point was not that wealth itself is bad but that it is dangerous. What starts out as a basic need for security too often becomes a continuing compulsive need for more, eventually including even the superfluous. This compulsive need is fed by a growing conviction that the wealthy person alone is responsible for all that is important in his or her life. Wealth becomes a false god. False gods do not satisfy, which is why divorce, substance abuse, and suicide rates are so high among the more affluent.

Is there anyone among you who would give his son a stone when he asked for bread? Or would hand him a snake when he asked for a fish?[221]

From Jesus' perspective, what is truly important are our relationships. And when I thought about the most positive changes in my life, they all involved new or improved relationships. God ensures we find, when our searching enables him to lead us in the right direction toward greater union with him, the source of all love. God is love. God calls us to love. God leads us to love.

Obviously, the reverse is also true. When, for whatever reason, we decide we have no interest in searching for more in our lives, we will stagnate. And start becoming less, for nothing stays the same. The choice is ours.

My second revelation involved what I had been thinking of as accidental encounters with fate. It finally occurred to me these accidental coincidences were not so accidental. God is a God of the unexpected. Father John Powell writes in his book *Seasons of the Heart*, "When God speaks (to us), there will always be something surprising, distinctive, and lasting."[222] In *Scattered Raindrops*, I

221 MT 7:9-10
222 *Seasons of the Heart, John Powell, SJ*, p. 187

168

defined these occurrences as miracles (any unexpected and unearned event that allows us to live life more fully[223]). Sometimes I think they are so numerous I should just call them blessings. In either case, I know my responsibility is to recognize and take advantage of these potential gifts.

And so, when I encountered a priest in New Hampshire who was clearly struggling with an overflow summer congregation, I asked if he would like some help, even though I was just there on vacation from our home in Boca Raton, Florida. He was so emphatic in his positive response that he unknowingly gave us just the push we needed to sell our Florida home and move to Frannie's family's summer home in New Hampshire. I have been serving in this (and its twinned Parish) ever since.

After my first full summer of helping at St. Joseph's in Ossipee, New Hampshire, the pastor, Father Tim O'Donnell, informed me he didn't have enough to keep me busy during the winter but would be glad to find me something at a larger Parish. However, the saltwater fly-fishing bug had bitten by then, so Frannie suggested we try a few weeks in the Florida Keys. That is how I met our good friend Father Tony Mullane and all the wonderful people at St. Peter's on Big Pine Key.

During those years, people would ask how we got so lucky to live part of the year in the Florida Keys and the rest of the year in New Hampshire. With a smile on my face, I would say, "I think it's God's will." Everyone who heard this answer inevitably laughed. They didn't realize I was serious.

We now live in a life care community called the Waterford in Juno Beach, Florida, still spending our summers in New Hampshire. We both had a hard time leaving St. Peter's, but on our second visit to what would become our new home, we attended the first Friday Mass held at the Waterford. Frannie loved the sermon given by the priest, Father Art Venezia.

During the luncheon that followed, someone asked Father Art what he was going to do now his assistant priest was leaving. He thought for a moment and said, "I've thought about it. If I could find just one Deacon who could help me out, I would be all right." Frannie and I looked at each other and knew it was another one of those moments. It would be another two years before we would actually make the move, by which time there already were two Deacons at St. Paul of the Cross. But we have loved our time there ever since. To

---

223 *Scattered Raindrops,* Deacon Bill Rich, p.102

this day, Father Art says he can't remember making that comment at lunch. But Frannie and I knew. "When God speaks (to us), there will always be something surprising, distinctive, and lasting."[224]

Give and you will receive.

I experienced this second promise because of the first. Seeking involves a good deal of sharing. And every time we shared we seemed to receive more than we gave. Many years ago we welcomed Chrissy and Claudie Montenegro and their mother Jeanne into our family. Today we count Chrissy and Claudie, their husbands, and their five children as our own. We gave to three. We now have nine. Whether raising a family or participating in Parish activities, we were giving and receiving, and it did not take long to realize something was changing in our lives. Which got me thinking about the "and you will receive" part. What were we receiving? And was it consistently greater than the effort we were expending?

I would like to use Jesus' parables to help answer these questions.

A King decides to forgive his servant's debts. The first servant owes the King a tremendous amount, let's say a million dollars, but despite this incredible debt, the King forgives him because the King is compassionate. This servant then meets a fellow servant who owes him one hundred dollars. The fellow servant pleads for mercy, just as the first servant had done with the King, but the first servant has him thrown into jail until the debt is paid. When the king hears about this, he withdraws his forgiveness from the first servant because he was not compassionate, and has him handed over to the torturers.[225]

Some construe this parable as an indication that God's forgiveness is conditional. God does not forgive unless we are willing to forgive.[226] I think Jesus was making a far different point. All of God's gifts, including the important gifts of his forgiveness and his love, must be opened. They must be accepted as part of the recipient's life for any benefit to be realized. So, "Do not judge, and you will not be judged; do not condemn and you will not be condemned; forgive and you will be forgiven"[227] means that as we refrain from judging others (only God judges people), we will become more accepting; as we refuse

---

224 *Seasons of the Heart, John Powell, SJ*, p. 187
225 MT 18:23-35
226 MT 18:35
227 LK 6:37

170

to condemn others, we will experience greater acceptance; as we forgive, we will know forgiveness. It's the way we are built. The way we were created. We become who we are.

The first way we receive is the reciprocal of what we have given. When I make the effort to heal, so am I healed.

Interestingly, what I have received has always seemed to be more than I have given. Increased comfort with myself and others, a greater sense of serenity, an ever-growing certainty that God and his love are real. Which may help explain the passage "Give, and there will be gifts for you: a full measure, pressed down, shaken together, running over, will be poured into your lap."[228]

But there is more.

In another parable, Jesus tells the story of a man about to go on a journey. He calls his servants together and gives them each some money: five talents to the first, two talents to the second, and one to the third. When he returns later, he calls the three into his presence and asks for an accounting.

The first servant (who was given five talents) proudly comes forward with ten. The master is impressed, saying, "Well done, good and trustworthy servant; you have been trustworthy in a few things; I will put you in charge of many things; enter the joy of your master." The second servant (who was given two talents) proudly comes forward with four. The master says exactly the same thing to him: "Well done, good and trustworthy servant; you have been trustworthy in a few things; I will put you in charge of many things; enter the joy of your master."

The third servant then comes forward and returns the one talent he was given. He acknowledges that he hid the talent in the ground because he was afraid of what the master might do if he lost it. The master has him thrown out and gives the talent to the servant with ten. Jesus concludes the parable by saying, "For to all those who have, more will be given, and they will have an abundance; but from those who have nothing, even what they have will be taken away."[229]

There are so many important insights in this parable! I think it is why I enjoy parables so much.

We are each given gifts or talents. Everyone has them, even those afraid to believe they do. When we use our talents, they become more, sometimes in terms of increased proficiency in the specific talent, sometimes in the acquisition of a related talent. Meaning we

228   LK 6:38
229   MT 25:14-29

become more. When I paint a lot, my painting gets better. When I cook a lot, my cooking gets better. When I do a lot of public speaking, my public speaking gets better. The last time I was doing a fair amount of public speaking, I became intrigued with singing and started taking lessons. I am sure you can think of similar examples in your own life.

The important point is not how many talents we start out with. The master says exactly the same thing to the servant who turns two talents into four as he does to the one who starts out with five and ends up with ten. The important point is that we be willing to use the talents God has given us. The important point is that we give of ourselves.

For when we give, we receive. Literally. We grow and become more. Think of the possibilities! If you are willing to devote the time and energy, think of what you can do in terms of realizing long-held dreams. So long as you do not let fear force you to bury your talents. Because "give and you will receive" also means you must give if you are to receive. Failure to do so cuts us off from sharing in the joy of the master.

Finally, Jesus concludes the parable by reminding his listeners that all choices have consequences. It is not simply a matter of giving or not giving. It is a question of whether we are growing or not growing. Giving of ourselves is the way we grow emotionally and spiritually. Nothing in this world remains the same. Everything is in the process of becoming more or less. Including us. I believe this includes the spiritual journey. I also believe Jesus would agree.

Which may be the reason Matthew follows this parable with the only description of the last judgment in the Gospels. The Son of Man returns in his glory, escorted by angels; takes his seat on his throne of glory; and proceeds to judge all the nations. Everyone is separated into two groups, referred to as the sheep on his right and the goats on his left. The only difference between the two groups is that those on his right have been willing to give of themselves, giving food to the hungry and drink to the thirsty, clothing the naked, visiting those in prison, making the stranger feel welcome. To these he says, "Come, you that are blessed by my Father, inherit the Kingdom prepared for you from the foundation of the world."[230]

> When we seek, we find
> Treasure beyond measure.

230   MT 25: 31-46

When we give, we receive
more of what we have given:
acceptance, forgiveness, love;
everything belongs.

When we give, we receive
talents that flourish,
birth to new growth;
mistakes mere lessons learned.

When we give, we receive
the priceless made real,
our search complete,
Kingdom as home.

Prayer

Luke 11:1–4

The Lord is near to all who call on him in truth.[231]

At several points in this book I have talked about the importance of our relationships. As the cornerstones of our emotional and spiritual well-being, their significance cannot be overstated.

All relationships depend on healthy communication. The willingness to describe our feelings while owning them, ask real versus superficial questions, risk touching what may hurt in an effort to heal, compliment goodness, acknowledge failings, and, at times most importantly, be willing to listen without being distracted. This is a tall order. Being a good communicator, particularly with loved ones, takes practice and patience, even for those who assume they are doing a good job. Meaningful relationships grow and become more when we work at communicating. They wither and die when we don't. It's that simple.

Prayer is the way we communicate in our relationship with God. Prayer helps us strengthen our bond with the Divine, fostering awareness of his caring touch in our lives. Just as with our human relationships, I think there is no such thing as a vibrant relationship with God without equally vibrant communication. Which means a healthy prayer life.

Roman Catholics tend to equate the word "prayer" with either formal prayer or prayers of petition.

Formal prayer means those prayers with the content pre-established, like the Our Father and the collection of prayers we call the Mass. Most of us think of these first because they are what we learned in our earliest religion classes, or are what we are exposed to when we go to church. Formal prayers hold great meaning even though they are often taken for granted. Most represent Jesus' teachings (e.g. the Our Father, parts of the Mass), God's continuing revelation in Tradition (e.g. the Creed, Hail Mary, the Divine Mercy Chaplet), or the inspiration of saints and early Church Fathers (e.g. parts of the Mass).

If you love someone who cherishes being addressed in a certain way, wouldn't you make the effort to do so? Formal prayer helps us do this in our relationship with God.

One very Catholic form of formal prayer is the Rosary. This prayer form is actually directed at both the Divine and Mary as

---

231 Psalm 145:18

our intercessor. Mary often refers to it in her visitations. As I have previously admitted, I get fidgety just thinking about the subject. I think it is an example of God's sense of humor that on most Fridays during the winter we participate in a communion service at our life care community where the participants like to conclude with the rosary.

Many find the rosary a particularly beneficial form of meditation, meaning a way to reflect on the mysteries of God's love. Those who seem to benefit most from the exercise feel a deep attraction to the Blessed Mother. I envy them. My suggestion for those interested is to give it a try with a more open mind than mine.

The other easily recognized prayer form, petitionary prayer, involves those times we are asking for help. Obviously, some prayers of petition also happen to be formal prayer (the Our Father contains six petitions), but in most cases our petitions are much more spontaneous. Asking for help is probably the most common prayer form, usually occurring when we or loved ones experience difficulty or danger.

Jesus encouraged prayers of petition (Ask and it will be given to you.[232] If in my name you ask me for anything, I will do it.[233] Very truly, I tell you, if you ask anything of the Father in my name, he will give it to you.[234]). So why does it seem that many prayers asking for help go unanswered?

One possible answer is that the God described by Jesus simply doesn't exist. I know this is not true because I have experienced the power of answered prayers. Seldom what I specifically requested. Almost never when I wanted. But almost always something better.

At the same time, I have wrestled with the fact that many prayers requesting some action on God's part appear to go unanswered. I am not sure why. If I ever have the opportunity to ask God, I plan to do so. In the meantime, I have chosen to believe the following:

- Too often my prayers of petition are based on little more than unexpected desperation. Metaphorically, I have come down with a headache and am looking for a gigantic aspirin to take away the pain. I pretend I am willing to trust in the goodness of God, because it is convenient to do so. These are not prayers; they are con games. Jesus

232 MT 7:7
233 JN 14:14
234 JN 16:23

had little patience with con games. He was most attracted to those willing to believe he had the power to help and were willing to trust in his goodness. These were the people who had faith. The Lord is near to all who call on him in truth.[235]

- God answers all my prayers. Often the answer is no. Sometimes for the reason mentioned above, often for a far better reason. I accept that God has a better idea than I do concerning what is best for me, as well as for those mentioned in my prayers. After all, God's ways are not our ways. For example, an unfortunate death to us may be in reality a loved one being brought to perfect happiness in union with the Divine.

- The closer my prayer is to God's will, the higher the probability I will be able to discern God's answer. So I often just take a shortcut in my petitions by praying for God's will. Something like "God, I turn my life over to you; help me to do as you would have me do, so I may know the joy and the peace of your Kingdom." Our friend Father Tony taught us another form of the same thing: "Sacred Heart of Jesus, I place all my trust in you." When I really want a specific outcome, such as relief for our daughter's fibromyalgia (long-term body-wide pain and fatigue), I ask for the specific and then conclude with "as in all things, your will, not mine, be done." I then do my best to try and mean what I have just said. I usually feel better just acknowledging God is in charge.

- Perhaps the best reason we do not think prayers are answered is we miss the major reason for praying. The following was written by Barbara Brown in her book *Bothering God* and was given to me after a Mass I attended recently in Johnson City, Tennessee. I am indebted for the gift and wish I had thought of what follows a long time ago.

In telling you how I understand prayer, I think right off that I will skip the usual stuff about how 'no' is a valid answer to prayer. As true as this may be, it sounds stingy to me. Even Jesus thought it

---

235   Psalm 145:18

stingy. "Is there anyone among you who, if your child asks for bread, will give a stone?"[236]

I think I will also stay away from the stuff about how we should only ask what accords with God's will. "Truly I tell you, if you say to this mountain 'Be taken up and thrown into the sea,' and if you do not doubt in your heart, but believe what you say will come to pass, it will be done for you."[237] Surely there are prayer requests more central to God's plan for you than rearranging the landscape.

What I want to share with you is that the best thing about prayer is the relationship itself. Whether or not you get what you ask for, I want you to keep asking; I want you to pester God like there is no tomorrow, thinking a dozen ways to plead your case. Remember the Gospel story about the persistent widow – that loud-mouthed woman who bothered an unjust judge until he gave her what she wanted. "And will not God grant justice to you the chosen ones who cry to him day and night?" Jesus asks his apostles at the end of the story. "Will God delay long in helping us?" [238] Well yes, God might. I am willing to concede that much. But there is more to prayer than the answer to prayer. There is also the pray-er, who is shaped by praying. What the persistent widow knows is that the most important time to pray is when your prayers seem meaningless. If you don't go and pester God like a widow, what are you going to do? Take to your bed with a box of Kleenex? Forget what matters to you altogether? No! Every day of your life, you are going to get up, wash your face, and go ask for what you want. You are going to trust the process, regardless of what comes from it, because the process of prayer gives you life.

One day, when we meet and you ask me outright whether prayer works, I'm going to say. "Oh, Sweetie, of course it does. It keeps our hearts chasing after God's heart. It's how we bother God, and how God bothers us back. There's nothing that works any better than that.[239]

Formal prayer and prayers of petition are the prayer forms most commonly recognized by Roman Catholics. If we limit ourselves to these, it would be like being in relationship with someone who never listened to what we had to say, and spent their time either ignoring us, spouting rehearsed lines, or asking for specific favors.

236   MT 7:9
237   MK 11:23
238   45 LK 18:7
239   *Bothering God*, Barbara Brown Taylor, published in the April/May issue of *Sacred Journey*

How long would such a relationship last? Fortunately, these prayer forms constitute but two parts of a much larger reality.

One of the most fruitful but overlooked prayer forms is what I will call conversation. Think of what goes into healthy conversation with someone you know. You make a point of saying something whenever you encounter each other. The greeting obviously varies depending on your mood, or what you are in the middle of, but there is still some form of recognition. If the person is someone you care for, you try to connect. Talk about what's going on in your life, express your feelings, including when they involve disappointment or frustration. You even take time to listen. At some level, you realize it is only when we are willing to share our whole selves, warts and all, are we really communicating.[240]

When we make the same effort with God, it can be a particularly meaningful form of prayer. Think of it as just talking about whatever is on your mind with someone you know cares immensely, will never take you for granted, and is always looking for ways to help.

One stumbling block to this kind of prayer is the often-expressed concern about expressing anger at the Divine or any form of doubt. My answer is this: How would you like to be in relationship with someone who refused to be honest with you? Besides, don't you think he already knows?

Talking with God increases our awareness of his presence in our lives. When such conversation becomes a habit, it makes it easier to see and be grateful for his contributions to our growth. To be less self, more God, centered.

A related prayer form is to consciously include the Divine in your creative activities. After all, we are called to be co-creators[241] in God's ongoing plan for bringing his creation to perfection. Creative activities most often thought of are related to the arts: music, painting, writing, quilting, and such. In actuality, any creative act, where you are making something that didn't exist before, including such things as gardening, creative cooking, or even just mediating on nature, qualify. The prayer involves letting go, allowing yourself to become fully engaged in your creative activity, so you, in my terms, become one with the Divine. From my own experience I can confirm that losing track of time, a cleansing of pressing concerns, even a sense of being refreshed, are common byproducts of such prayer.

---

240   *Seasons of the Heart*, John Powell, SJ, p.240
241   Catechism, 306-308

There are other ways to pray, especially in relation to the Holy Scripture. I encourage you to look for ways to pray that resonate with you. Remember, seek and you will find. As part of our discussion in this book, I would like to focus on just one more prayer form, the one that has had the most dramatic effect on my life.

There is a centuries-old tradition in our Church called contemplative prayer, which can be defined as living life with a conscious awareness of the Divine. I think this comes from a habit of conversing with God, AND a willingness to listen to God in a structured way. One approach to doing so is called centering prayer. Father Thomas Keating, credited by some with founding the centering prayer movement and author of the book *Open Mind Open Heart,* refers to it as pure faith.[242] I like to think of it as taking time to listen to God. Listening is one of the most important forms of communication in any loving relationship.

There is an interesting story in the first Book of Kings in the Old Testament. Elijah is fleeing from Ahab, who is attempting to kill all the prophets. He arrives at Horeb, the mountain of God, where he hides in a cave. During the night, a voice tells him God is about to pass by. Elijah hears a great wind that splits mountains and breaks rocks. But the Lord is not in the wind. Then an earthquake occurs, but the Lord is not in the earthquake. Then a fire, and once again the Lord is not there. Finally, Elijah hears a "sound of sheer silence." Knowing the Lord is now present, he walks to the mouth of the cave and encounters his God.[243]

Have you ever wondered why Jesus' disciples asked him to teach them how to pray?[244] The answer lies in examining how Jesus himself prayed. At multiple points in the Gospels, Jesus goes off by himself to do just that. His most common prayer form was solitary, where he could commune with his Father. His followers wanted a formal spoken prayer similar to what they had heard John's disciples using.[245] Small wonder, then, that they had to ask for his help; they had never been part of his personal prayer. In fact, in Matthew's account of Jesus' instruction on prayer, he says, "When you pray, go

---

242 *Open Heart, Open Mind* by Rev. Thomas Keating, provided my introduction to centering prayer. I am indebted to Keating. What is presented here would not have been possible without his influence and I credit him for what is contained in this book.

243 1 Book of Kings 19: 3, 9, 11-13

244 MT 6: 7-13; LK 11:1-4

245 LK 11: 1

into your private room, shut yourself in, and so pray to your Father who is in that secret place."[246]

Centering prayer is one way to go off by yourself to your secret place so you can commune with the Lord. It is not a form of yoga, relaxation exercise, or mystical undertaking. It is a simple but disciplined way to consciously open yourself to the Divine. To center yourself on the Divine. So you may experience "pure faith."

The mechanics of centering prayer are straightforward. Go off by yourself to a quiet and comfortable place. I have found my study first thing in the morning to be best for me. Every hour I delay my centering prayer decreases by fifty percent the chances I will do it that day. The few times I have added a second session of centering prayer in the late afternoon or early evening, I have found it more difficult to maintain my focus. Perhaps that is because of an almost irresistible urge to fall asleep.

I make myself comfortable by lying down on a day bed. Most people would probably be better off in a comfortable chair, but I have a circulatory problem in my legs that causes almost constant fidgeting when I am in a seated position. I close my eyes, say a brief opening prayer ("Thank you, Jesus"), and empty my mind. I try to think of nothing. I am Elijah listening for a "sound of sheer silence."[247] I am consciously opening myself to the Divine by listening to the language of God: the sound of sacred silence. I do this for thirty minutes every day, although a beginner may want to start with twenty. A quiet alarm clock (no tick tick tick) easily solves the problem of knowing when to end the prayer session.

About twenty to thirty seconds into your first attempt, you will discover a disconcerting fact. Thoughts are occurring, despite your best intentions. They seem to be flowing by, like rubbish in a river. The first reaction is to try harder, then get irritated, and then decide there must be easier ways to pray.

Why is it so difficult to control or even influence what our mind is doing?

There are several answers to this question. My favorite one involves defense mechanisms developed early in life (false self) to protect the fragile sense of self (true self). The true self is the loving and trusting self that God intends us to be. The problem occurs when the false self does not want to give up control when it is no longer needed by the maturing adult. And so it keeps diverting us away

246   MT 6: 6
247   1 Book of Kings 19: 12

from any activity that strengthens and encourages the ascendancy of the true self.[248] I like this explanation because it is what I have experienced with centering prayer.

The first lesson and primary lesson in centering prayer involves accepting the goal is not an empty mind but dealing with unwanted thoughts. The former tends to occur once the latter is accomplished. There are two ways to do this. First, decide on a short phrase (once again, mine is "Thank you, Jesus") that becomes your nonconscious way of saying, "I want to reenter sacred silence." Second, when unwanted thoughts start to float by in your mind, do not get irritated or frustrated or discouraged. Relax (a way of accepting their reality), patiently say your phrase, gently let go of the thought, and return to your sacred silence. Never condemn or try to judge your lack of success. Just gently try again. Be persistent. God's ways are not our ways. Two or three brief interludes of relaxed waiting on the Lord in your thirty minutes of trying may be enough.

You will soon find there are some days the process seems much easier and other days when you feel that you will never "get it." Just be patient. If necessary, forgive yourself. And then persevere. Thank you, Jesus.

Before long (measured in months for me, but it may be different for you) the benefits of centering prayer will start to appear. The first indication will be when you realize the habits you are forming in your prayer life (increased acceptance, patience, willingness to let go, and persistence) are spreading to the rest of your life. I found this to be particularly true with letting go of the unimportant. You may even find yourself more forgiving. I don't know how long this transformation continues. In my case, it just seems to keep getting better.

The next thing you might notice is unwanted thoughts become less random and more important. Thinking of something you have forgotten to do, sudden inspiration regarding a potential way to solve a problem, even a pleasing sensation that prompts you to think "I must be experiencing the Divine" are but three examples. For a while I would stop my centering prayer to write down these important thoughts. When I looked at them later, I almost always wondered why they had seemed so important. Then, thanks to a chapter in Father Keating's book, I realized what was happening. I was making progress. What I chose to call my false self was fighting back because

---

248   *Wikipedia*

it was losing control. I was becoming more comfortable being the person God had always wanted me to be.

Finally, there are benefits of centering prayer that gently surface over time. I like to think of these as the gifts of the Holy Spirit:

- Feeling completely relaxed during centering prayer, knowing you are in the presence of something much greater than any of your worries, fears or concerns (Father Keating calls this 'resting in the Lord').
- The urge to laugh more often, worry less.
- Greater intuitive insight into the next right thing to do. Increased compassion, the ability to see and enter the chaos of another.
- An overwhelming sense of humility, knowing it really is good to be me, because between God and me, there is nothing we cannot overcome.

God is good.
He patiently waits for us to open,
so he can enter
and,
if we let him,
lead us to fulfillment.
God is good.
So good.

Pruning

John 15:1–11

One of the ways John's Gospel differs from the other three is Jesus' use of several images to describe himself. Bread of Life, Living Water, and the Good Shepherd are but a few examples. Using images familiar to his listening audience, Jesus highlighted his relationship with his Father and, at the same time, the power his Father had given him to help us live more satisfying lives. The inspiration for this discussion comes from one of these images: the true vine.

Jesus begins by establishing his relationship to his Father. He is the vine; the Father is the vine grower. He comes from the Father, and all his power has its source in this intimate connection. He then defines his relationship to us. He is the vine; we are the branches. He is the true vine because only through our connection to him can we enjoy eternal life (in John's Gospel, eternal life is joy based life beginning as soon as we are connected to Jesus).

When we remain or abide in Jesus, meaning when we make the effort to live life as he asks us to, Jesus will remain or live within us, helping us on our journey. We will then bear much fruit, meaning we will live life more fully. Bearing fruit will glorify God because the glory of God is a person fully alive.[249] God will prune the branches that bear fruit so they can bear even more fruit.

Oops.

What's that about being pruned? That sounds painful, like something to be avoided. Couldn't we just pretend that line wasn't there?

But if we did, would we also have to discard the last line in this passage: "I have said these things to you so that my joy may be in you and your joy may be complete"?[250]

We human beings have an aversion to change. Sometimes we find sufficient internal motivation to change on our own, like losing weight to become healthier or more attractive. But I submit that almost all significant change occurs in our life when we experience discomfort. Pruning is the discomfort in our lives.

For every one person who comes to me wanting to know about growing spiritually because it seems like a good idea, ten come because they can think of no other way to eliminate the pain in their lives. This pain is almost never physical. It is almost always related

---

249   St. Irenaeus
250   JN 15:11

to the religious question (isn't there more to life?) or a relationship problem.

William Bridges, author of the book *The Way of Transition,* argues that change is critically important to our well-being but often difficult because people resist transitions, meaning change that involves "the process of letting go of the way things used to be and then taking hold of the way they subsequently become," passing through a "chaotic but potentially creative 'neutral zone' along the way."[251] I think this is perceptive, because all meaningful change involves transition. In *Scattered Raindrops,* I referred to this process as the cycle of life, dying to what was and rising to new life, with a difficult but meaningful period in between. There is no growth of the human spirit and the human being without transitions. Interestingly, when we are in transition, we experience doubt and periods of disorientation, but it is also when we are most completely alive.[252] I believe almost all transitions are undertaken because of pain. In its own way, each transition is a gift. It is the way we grow into new life...after being pruned. It is our choice.

While one may debate whether the afflicted are comforted, it is clear the comfortable are afflicted.[253]

One of the most important lessons in Scripture deals with making the most of transitions. The lesson is this: Trust God will lead you to new life; trust even when understanding fails. Think of the biblical heroes responsible for the greatest positive change: Jesus, Mary and Joseph, Paul, the Apostles, the Prophets, Moses, and Abraham, to name ones that come to mind quickly. Each one of their stories is a story of transition in the face of almost insurmountable difficulty. In every case they trusted in the goodness of God, often without understanding how their situation could possibly end positively. And in every case, their transition resulted in new life for themselves and countless others.

Obviously, this business of trusting in God is easier said than done. Particularly since there is the possibility God is responsible

---

251   *The Way of Transition,* William Bridges, p. 2. For those who would like to know more about transitions, I recommend reading William Bridges' *The Way of Transition.* It is an informative humanistic analysis of the subject.
252   *The Way of Transition*, William Bridges, p.85
253   *Wikipedia,* Anonymous Quote, most often attributed to Mother Mary Jones and Finley Peter   Dunne

for whatever is troubling us. After all, isn't God the one doing the pruning?

You are free to decide whatever you want on this question. After a good deal of thought on the subject I have decided I believe the following:

- God is almighty, meaning he is sustaining and evolving his creation. Nothing exists without him. Beyond that, he does interact with us in our daily lives, nudging us toward decisions that will lead us to fulfillment. In this process God respects our free will. The choice is ours.
- Life happens, which means there is a randomness to life that provides plenty of occasions for pruning. Life helps us grow, presenting opportunities for transitions to new life. Seldom is God responsible for specific problems in our lives. We do a good job of that all on our own.
- No matter what happens to us, God will always lead us to new life if we make the effort to do our part and learn to trust in his goodness.

In my experience, the most painful transition involves the unexpected loss of a loved one. Believing life and love are eternal may help intellectually, but it seldom eases the almost indescribable pain. The most others can usually do is be present to the person going through this tormenting transition called grieving.

A volunteer at St. Peter's in the Florida Keys named Mary Quirk helped me understand grief. She taught me it is a process, a natural transition that helps one heal the end of a lost relationship while creating new ones, often with a richer and deeper perspective on life. It is a process that can literally take years, and the one grieving is the only one who can go through it. This person will never be the same, but whether that means more or less complete depends upon the individual. In particular, it depends on whether the individual is willing to make the effort.

Anyone over twenty years old can point to other examples of pruning in their own lives. One of the great privileges of being a permanent deacon is the opportunity to share in these transitions, particularly those that end in death. This may sound odd, but they are almost always inspirational examples of the beauty of the human spirit and the power of God's love.

Rather than talk about these, I would like to share several examples from my own life. They are not particularly unique, but they are mine. We all have been pruned.

Dealing with my alcoholism is probably my most striking experience of transitioning from a self-created hell to new life. Since I have already covered this, as well as my cancer, let me touch on several others.

Remember my talking about the power of centering prayer in my life? What I didn't mention is that I stopped after almost two years of integrating this prayer form into my life. I am not even sure why. And I didn't restart, even though I could feel the resulting emptiness.

About a year later, I contracted a unique skin disease called recalcitrant palmoplantar psoriasis, a chronic (meaning incurable) recurring (meaning it keeps coming back) condition that affects the palms of the hands and the soles of the feet. In practical terms, it means the skin on my palms and the bottom of my feet hardens and cracks, with the risk of inflammation and infection.

It took over a year to get an accurate diagnosis, by which time I had so infected my two thumbs while saltwater fly-fishing that the doctor threatened to hospitalize me. With the help of two specialists over the next twelve months, I learned that application of three different salves twice a day could control the symptoms. What choice did I have? I wanted the discomfort to stop.

Now here's the humorous part. These three different salves come as either creams (meaning they disappear quickly when applied) or ointments (which means they don't). Ointments are more effective than creams. This means that I must spend thirty minutes twice a day in a reclining position (sound vaguely familiar?), with these ointments on my stationary hands and feet. Frannie calls it my dead dog pose.

I have had this condition for seven years. I returned to centering prayer about six years ago. When asked if I am bothered by my psoriasis, I am not sure how to answer the question. I am grateful for my centering prayer. Other than that, the question has no meaning. I cannot choose to end my psoriasis, and there is no other viable treatment option. As a result, I choose to view my psoriasis as an opportunity to pray every morning and spend time with my wife every evening. I have never regretted this choice.

I think the most difficult time in my life occurred when we discovered my wife had breast cancer. The uncertainty as we waited for a final diagnosis, the operation, and then the follow-up radiation were almost unbearable. I don't think I have ever been so disoriented. I was faced with the prospect of losing her. When we finally learned she would be all right I burst into tears. To this day, I am not sure how I would deal with her death.

Reflecting on this experience led to changes in my life. When dealing with someone with a serious or life-threatening illness, I now try to remember that the caregiver also faces a challenging, and sometimes more difficult, time. When I shared this with Frannie, she admitted my cancer experience had been much more difficult for her than going through her own.

In my relationship with my wife, I try to let the memory of what I experienced during her cancer treatment help me overlook unimportant hurts or irritations. I focus instead on what sustains our relationship, trying to be grateful for the good times we share. I know this may sound simplistic, but it works. Transitions caused by pruning lead to new life.

I am getting older. As part of that process I have discovered there are certain things I used to enjoy tremendously (such as hunting chukar partridges with my older brother in mountainous terrain, or ten-day biking trips with my wife) that are either much harder or unsafe. I have also discovered I accomplish less each day than I used to. I kiddingly tell people I now know so much it takes me longer to remember any one specific, but I think the real reason is I need more rest. And then there's the almost endless list of pills to be ingested. I have discovered that aging causes its own discomforts, and I am not referring just to arthritis.

Frannie and I have also found aging is an opportunity. Obviously, it is better than the alternative. In addition, embracing the transition rather than fighting it has led to a lifestyle we had hardly thought possible. As mentioned earlier, our primary residence is now in a wonderful life care community called The Waterford in Southern Florida. When we joined we were the youngest people there. We love the friends we have made, as well as the freedom of letting someone else prepare meals and clean our apartment. We have also discovered we are more comfortable in a smaller and simpler living space.

I no longer bird hunt. But my fly-fishing (which does not require either the stamina or the balance) has blossomed. Frannie and I love our almost daily biking on the level bike paths in Florida. We are even planning our first cruise. And we have more time and energy to spend on our ministry, grandkids, painting, and quilting. I can't remember when I have been happier.

Life happens.
It's part of God's plan.
Pruning gives us the opportunity
to choose new life.
Transitions leading home
to joy.

Choosing Joy

John 15:11

In the first chapter of this book I discussed how I experience joy in my own life. Now I would like to discuss joy from a different standpoint. Specifically, I would like to focus on our ability to choose joy.

The word "joy" is mentioned one hundred seventy-eight times in the Bible; the word rejoice another one hundred and forty five. It doesn't take an expert to realize there must be some connection between God and joy. What is it?

I am sure those of us who were raised in the 1940s and 1950s might suspect a scam. Weren't we taught that love of God meant we must work at living perfect lives in complete obedience to God, the Church, our priest, and, if present, the nuns? In return for which we would, if judged to be acceptable by Jesus, experience an ill-defined everlasting joy in heaven?

I think Scripture is trying to tell us something far more profound.

There are many ways to describe joy. The dictionary definition is a feeling of great pleasure and happiness.[254] I have taken liberties with a quote from the Jesuit priest John Powell[255] to come up with my own definition: A radical (meaning unqualified) self-acceptance that results in an interior sense of celebration. The great mythologist Joseph Campbell simply called it bliss. In any case, the sensation of joy is always triggered by something, usually the choices you or I make (I can't just decide to feel joy; there must be a cause). In addition, joy is a positive, life-giving force. I can experience an adrenalin rush when I get angry or exact revenge or take a shortcut to what I think is happiness, but that is not joy. Joy is always positive and is always life-giving.

Some feelings of great pleasure and happiness result from conscious choices we make: our wedding, the birth of our children, specific job successes, even a painting turning out better than expected. More often, however, they just happen, almost always when we experience an unexpected and unearned event in our lives that allows us to live life more completely. The chance meeting of someone who helps us love more fully (how did you meet the person most important to you in your life?), someone helping find what you

---

254 New Oxford American Dictionary
255 *Seasons of the Heart,* John Powell, S.J., p. 102

feared lost, a beautiful sunrise after a good night's sleep; these are but a few examples.

Usually we refer to these occurrences as coincidences. I prefer to think of them as God's blessings. Think of the times you have said, "What a blessing!' or "I feel so blessed." Isn't it almost always after something unexpected and unearned has happened that enriches your life?

Regardless of how much or little choice is involved in these times of great pleasure and happiness, they are almost always fleeting in duration. Without realizing it, we soon find ourselves immersed once again in the ongoing drama of daily life. Fortunately, the memories of these moments stay with us. They become a pool of goodness, providing a temporary lift to help us transcend the more mundane parts of life.

God created us with this capacity. We are wired for joy. God's will is for us to experience joy, building an ever-growing wellspring of goodness that eventually will culminate in union with the source of all joy. Fleeting feelings of great pleasure and happiness are a foretaste of what is to come.

The "Gifts" covered in the previous chapter can be causes for joy. Whenever I find a new home where I feel accepted as I am, discover I am able to emulate Mary for a short period of time, experience a sudden new insight into Scripture or the wonder of the Real Presence, I feel joyful...meaning I am filled with joy for several moments. When we take time to accept life's gifts as the gifts they truly are, we open ourselves to joy.

For some time I wondered if this was all that what was meant by references to joy in Scripture.

Several years ago, my brother and I, along with our wives, traveled to South Bend, Indiana, for a Notre Dame football game. The Friday before the game was a first Friday, so my brother and I attended Mass at the Parish church where our father's memorial Mass had been held. I can't remember what the readings were, but the priest giving the homily brought me to full attention when, after reflecting on the challenges of being a caring priest, he asked, "What is joy?" After a long pause, he said softly but with great conviction, "Joy is a call rightly lived." He then went on to comment on the deep satisfaction he felt living his call to the priesthood.

When I am unsettled by something, I have a hard time thinking of much else until I decide why I am bothered. In this case, I soon realized my initial reaction that the priest was rationalizing his decision to become a priest was slowly giving way to an epiphany for me (a moment of sudden insight or revelation). My deepest and most enduring sense of well-being came not so much from moments of great pleasure or happiness. It came from my marriage, helping raise my children, and my diaconate ministry—activities that gave me a sense of purpose in life. All three were primarily long-term commitments to work at building relationships. In the priest's vernacular, they were calls rightly lived.

While all three have included moments of great pleasure, they also have included times of disappointment, anger, and frustration. There have been failures and setbacks. All three have required perseverance and a willingness to respond positively to being pruned, not once but multiple times. Because at the heart of a call rightly lived is a willingness to heed Jesus' call to "follow me," leaving where we are emotionally, mentally, and even spiritually to travel uncharted roads. So we can find joy.

A call defines you. When asked who I am, I answer without thinking. A husband, a father, a permanent deacon. I am proudest of, and get the most satisfaction from, my marriage, my children, and my diaconate. I think this kind of joy is close to shalom, the word Jesus used when saying, "Peace be with you." Shalom means peace, completeness, well-being, and safety.[256] Think of constructive self-acceptance, resulting in an interior sense of celebration.

How does God fit into this expanded definition of joy? To start with, if a call is a call, someone is doing the calling. God calls each of us to live life more completely by using the gifts he has given us and by making choices about which attitudes we emphasize, the way we see, our willingness to heal and so on. God communicates this call in multiple ways, including a feeling of satisfaction with certain activities, the ability to imagine doing more of the same, and those seeming coincidences that make such dreaming possible.

During the Christmas season, we celebrate the feast of Epiphany, when wise men followed a star to find the newborn King. This was their call. They were wise because they were willing to respond to the call, using God's guidance to find their way. Their epiphany was realizing that the newborn babe in very humble surroundings was indeed the King they had been seeking. A call rightly lived. No wonder the story resonates across so many cultures. It is meant to be our story.

---

256   Wikipedia

As I was preparing my notes for this part of the book, our son Bill and his wife visited us one weekend. Bill was reading a book called *The Element*. In response to my question concerning its contents, he said he was looking for thoughts that might help him in his profession as a high school teacher. I smiled, made some noncommittal comment, and started to turn my attention back to my notes, until he added, "It's about finding what makes you happy."

Needless to say, I got a copy of the book and consumed it. I was struck by how the author, Dr. Ken Robinson, had unwittingly contributed to my reflection on the subject of choosing joy, for his conclusions reinforced and expanded my own thinking.

At the risk of doing Dr. Robinson an injustice, I would like to share what struck me most forcefully from my reading of *The Element*.

The element is the intersection of our aptitude (what we are good at) with what we enjoy (and therefore can become passionate about). Both our aptitudes and what we can become passionate about are part of our makeup as unique human beings. As such, they are free gifts given us by our Creator, meaning we can chose to develop them (or not), but we did nothing to earn or deserve them.

The book is filled with short case studies of famous people finding their element. Dr. Robinson's intent is not to imply that only famous people can find their element. In fact, he uses the stories to make just the opposite point: we can all find our element if we are willing to seek what we can become passionate about. Joseph Campbell said it slightly differently. He encouraged those trying to discern their future to follow their bliss.

If God is real, if God is love, if God calls and leads us to love, it only makes sense to me he would give each of us a way to more fully experience joy in our lives.

Finding our element often takes incredible work, including a willingness to think for oneself, resist social pressures to conform, and persevere in the face of life's ever-present obstacles. We can choose to persevere, trusting our intuition (God's gentle encouragement to follow our star), knowing that setbacks are really lessons learned along the way to eventual fulfillment. We can choose to seek, confident we will find. Just follow your bliss.

It is difficult to exaggerate the importance of our attitudes in finding and fully exploiting our element. The biggest obstacle is an attitude of fear: fear of failure, fear of leaving our comfort zones, or fear of being ridiculed. Many people who successfully find their element decide to "feel the fear but do it anyway."[257] And grow in the process. They also maintain an attitude of openness toward new possibilities and the counsel of mentors. Finally, a positive attitude toward self (constructive self-acceptance) and toward life (thinking you are lucky often results in being lucky) is especially helpful.

When we are in our element, we are completely engaged and so energized that other parts of our lives are transformed, making life itself more meaningful. As we change, our perception of the world around us changes. We experience a deep sense of self-worth and well-being (an interior sense of celebration).

Finding and pursuing one's element are independent of age. People in their fifties, sixties, seventies and even eighties have found and been transformed by being in their element. In addition, our element may be a life-consuming vocation or multiple activities that give add depth, balance, and meaning to our lives. This makes great sense to me. If you loved someone to the depths of your being, wouldn't you want that person to have the opportunity to experience joy at any age and in many ways?

While I have never talked with Dr. Robinson, I am almost certain he never intended his work to be referenced in a book about the connection between God and joy. Please accept the interpretations of what he has written as mine alone. I have also said nothing about many other meaningful and complementary points in the book, which is well worth reading. I continue to marvel that it made its appearance in my life just when I could take advantage of it.

I would like to conclude with a story, the story of our son Tim.

Tim is our youngest son. He was an energetic boy with multiple crosses to bear, including an older brother who seemed to do everything right, a father who was often too busy to show affection, and an intermittent learning disability that prevented certain information from reaching his brain. The testing that confirmed this fact left Timmy complaining, "I'm just a retard."

Tim was bright without recognizing it. He was athletic without working to take advantage of his gifts. He was a wonderfully affectionate human being who seemed to go out of his way to prove otherwise. He constantly found himself in trouble. Tim had inherited one of my most important traits, my alcoholism.

I won't bore you with the details of Tim's journey through his disease. He did do well at a sales job after high school graduation, proclaiming it was his destiny to make so much money he would be

257   *The Element,* Dr. Ken Robinson, p.190

happy. He also went to college, essentially on his own. It took him five years, and he displayed a capacity for dedicated effort seldom seen before. When he graduated, he had the following words pasted to the top of his mortarboard: TODAY, HELL FROZE OVER.

Tim's drinking and drugging finally cost him a good job, his marriage, his home, and the vast majority of his friends. He was completely alone in a hell of his own making. But then he decided to change. He had asked the religious question.

Almost penniless, he committed himself to getting back on his feet. He started going to AA meetings, where he discovered a higher power he chooses to call God, as well as a new set of friends willing to go to almost any length to help him. Tim had found a home.

Over the next two years, Tim stuck to his guns, making just enough money to survive at a variety of part-time jobs, slowly rising to new life. He dared to start thinking about his future, deciding he would become a teacher because he had always enjoyed working with children. Undaunted by the almost surmountable odds faced by an unemployed man in his late thirties, he went back to college to get the credits needed for a teacher preparation program in Vermont. His brother Bill and Bill's wife, Emily, both active teachers, provided him priceless advice, eventually inviting him to come live with them in their home outside Burlington, Vermont, while he got on his feet.

When his application to the teacher preparation program was rejected, Tim could have consoled himself with any of several reasons for giving up. But he did not. He persevered. With Bill and Emily's encouragement, he decided to move to Vermont and live with Bill and Emily for as long as a year. He would use the time to find a job while he took additional education courses.

Almost by coincidence, he took a minimal paying job as a teacher's aide for disadvantaged children in the school system ten minutes from Bill and Emily's home. Here, Tim's aptitude (working with kids) intersected with what he discovered made him very happy (special education). He had found his element. He had experienced joy.

Today, Tim is in his own apartment, attending a master's program for special education at the University of Vermont. He works a full-time job to support himself. He also finds time for his AA program and for volunteer work at a local hospital. He says he loves it because it makes him feel better. He has never been happier.

Tim continues to have his share of problems, but they are good problems. In many ways, he is still recovering from the emotional stunting caused by substance abuse. He has many friends, but I am sure, at some level, he would love to be a husband again and a father for the first time. Finally, who knows if he will succeed in his chosen field? But I am incredibly proud of him. I thank God for answered prayers, and I would never bet against him. For he has experienced joy as a sober sibling and son, as a contributing member of his AA home, and in the pursuit of his element.

The transforming effect of being in our element adds a new dimension to the idea of a call rightly lived. In addition to calling us to lifestyles that encourage beneficial relationships, God calls us to use our talents to create more. So we can be fully engaged in and passionate about life. And when we make the effort to do so, God whispers, "Well done, good and trustworthy servant; enter the joy of your master."[258] For "to all those who have, more will be given, and they will have an abundance."[259]

Joy is real. Joy is God-given. We are wired for joy. Joy is a choice.

For those of you who still have never experienced true joy,

Be not afraid,[260]
O, you of little faith.[261]
I came so you might have life, and have it abundantly.[262]
Do not worry.[263]
My yoke is easy and my burden light.[264]
Follow me.[265]
I tell you this
so my joy may be in you,
and your joy may be complete.[266]

---

258   MT 25:21
259   MT 25:29
260   Repeated twenty-six times in the four Gospels.
261   MK 14:27
262   JN 10:10
263   MT 6:34
264   MT 11:30
265   LK 5:27
266   JN 15:11

Summary

Choices, as used here, represent God's gifts that require more active participation on our part. They are free gifts because we have done nothing to deserve them. However, we must make the effort to take advantage of them. Unlike the gifts discussed previously, our failure to make the effort usually results in reduced freedom to live our lives to the fullest extent. All choices have consequences.

The following choices are not all-inclusive. They represent merely the ones I have found most beneficial. I hope they will help you think of other examples in your own lives.

Attitudes

Our attitudes are similar to our feelings, with one important exception. We can consciously decide what our attitudes will be. Positive attitudes help us grow by changing the way we view life, which in turn improves our emotional reaction to events in our lives.

Obviously, negative attitudes like unhealthy anger, shame, and remorse do just the reverse.

The Beatitudes describe the most important attitudes. These "love attitudes" are humility, compassion, forgiveness, and righteousness.

Seeing

Early in life we are trained to learn to discern differences by comparing, and to believe what we can confirm with our five senses or through logical analysis. Such rational thinking has led to most of the material advances in our society, as it is very helpful for abstract thinking.

It has also inculcated in us a tendency for "either/or" seeing, which tends to lead to all-or-nothing, exclusionary, and even "better than/less than" thinking. The biggest drawback is that much of life is not "either/or." All of God's creation and our existence within it are "both/and."

"Both/and" seeing helps us acquire a more realistic and compassionate view of life and ourselves. It also helps us more fully appreciate the great mysteries, which often are the most important parts of life.

Most important Roman Catholic Traditions are based on "both/and" thinking. Jesus was arguably the greatest "both/and" teacher.

Healing

Many of Jesus' healing miracles had a particular pattern: a willingness to care, reach out, and touch what hurt despite the risk, wanting only what was best for the person in need. Whenever there was openness to this approach, there was a cure (change in the physical or mental makeup) and a healing (restoration of relationship).

Few have the power to cure. We all have the power to heal when we are willing to follow this pattern. As we heal, so are we healed.

Promises

Holy Scripture demonstrates that God is a promise maker. God's promises are all variations of the great promise in the Exodus story. If we commit ourselves to be his people, making his ways our ways, he will lead us from whatever enslaves us to the Promised Land: joy in finding our way home.

Two of God's promises are "Seek and you will find" and "Give and you will receive." Both have the power to dramatically change our lives if we choose to take advantage of them.

Prayer

All relationships grow or wither depending on the quality of their communication. Prayer is the way we communicate with the Divine. A healthy relationship with God is built on a vibrant prayer life.

There are many forms of prayer. Formal prayer, petitions, conversational prayer, and co-creator prayer are examples of common prayer forms.

The most effective petition is to pray for the grace to do God's will.

God answers all prayers.

A particularly powerful prayer form called "centering prayer" is premised on listening to God in sacred silence.

Pruning

God is the vine grower. Jesus is the vine. We are the branches. The vine grower prunes branches so they will produce more fruit.

Pruning is discomfort we experience that leads to positive change. God is responsible for pruning in the sense he is responsible for a creation in which life happens.

All meaningful change involves transitions, unsettled times when we let go of what was in order to embrace what will be.

When we make the effort to change and trust in God's goodness, he will always lead us to a new life. Obviously, the reverse is also true.

It is our choice.

Choosing Joy

Joy is a life-giving, positive reality.

Joy is God-given.

There are different forms of joy, including spontaneous moments of great pleasure, a call rightly lived, and being in one's element.

We are wired for joy.

Joy is a choice.

VII
The Future

For Our Church

One of the questions I am often asked is "What do you think our Church will be like in the future?"

Clearly there are a number of issues being debated concerning the future of the Catholic Church. I am not speaking here of the sexual abuse scandal. There is near-unanimous agreement on what went wrong and what should be done. I am talking about issues facing the Church that are still in search of a consensus, like the role of women in the Church hierarchy, an all-celibate priesthood, artificial contraception, and teachings on homosexuality. This list is not meant to be all-inclusive.

In my opinion, these issues represent the centuries-long clash between well-intended defense of the past and well-intended hope for the future. I believe this is a healthy tension and will continue to exist as long as the Roman Catholic Church exists. This belief is premised on my view that the tension is dialectical, meaning that the clash between two opposing points of view will produce a better answer than would be produced by either side on its own. I think continued disagreement and dialogue are what will eventually lead to helpful change in our Church.

I also believe in a lesson from the Acts of the Apostles. Gamaliel, a teacher of the law respected by all the people, provided the following counsel to his fellow council members who wanted to kill the apostles: "If this plan or undertaking is of human origin, it will fail; but if it is of God, you will not be able to overthrow them—in that case you may even be found fighting against God!"[267]

In my judgment, not one of these issues is as important as what I perceive to be the central crisis facing Roman Catholicism: an unaddressed spiritual hunger that has led to the loss of so many and has little to do with what we Catholics spend most of our time arguing about. In my opinion, resolution of all the issues I have mentioned as those recommending significant change would like will do little to address this crisis. For those of you who might disagree, I suggest you examine the mainstream traditional Protestant churches.

I have tried to focus my energies on activities that might help satisfy that spiritual hunger, at least to some small extent. The best place to do this, in my judgment, is within the Parish structure.

When Hispanic immigrants are not considered, the only Christian faith traditions growing rapidly are what I refer to as more

---

267   Acts, 7: 38-39

traditional mega-churches. I use the term "more traditional" because the theology preached is not fundamentalist. With the exception of our sacramental emphasis and belief in apostolic succession, it is surprisingly similar to what Roman Catholics hear. What makes these churches unique is their passion to make religion relevant in today's world, an emphasis on addressing the needs of parishioners, and a fearless promotion of tithing (a biblically based commitment to give ten percent of your annual "first fruits" to charity). As a priest friend of mine says, "Peoples' hearts are where their treasure is, and I want their hearts."

Frannie and I have had the privilege to participate in three Parish communities that were alive with this kind of spirit. All three felt like home, where we received far more than we gave. All three had pastors willing to foster change by encouraging the laity to do more. Only one of these pastors was what I would call charismatic or an inspired speaker. All three did possess a strong Gospel-based faith, an open heart, and an aversion to being judgmental.

Newcomers felt welcome and were quickly invited to take a more active part in the Parish. This would come from another parishioner rather than a bulletin announcement and would almost always start with a request to be part of a short-term, one-time project. In a surprising number of cases, this beginning would then lead to some form of continuing involvement. I chuckle saying all this, thinking of my own reconnection with the Catholic Church through a priest offering to play basketball on a weekday night, with the implied offer of a few beers afterwards.

Parish activities in these three Parishes would include a healthy balance between purely social and more spiritually oriented ministries. Emphasis on addressing parishioners' real needs, reverence for the Sacraments, and at least one annual Parish retreat were present in each case. Some form of outreach to the less fortunate was always paramount. A sure sign of someone finding a sense of home in one of these Parishes would be his or her reaction when someone criticized "the Church." He or she would take it personally. People cared for each other and for their Parish. It was their Church.

American writer Paul Wilkes, best known for his focus on religion, published a book on *Excellent Catholic Parishes: The Guide to Best Places and Practices*. Two things struck me about the Parishes he covered. The first was that the only things all the Parishes had in common were a commitment to being relevant, an active laity, and a vibrant spirituality. Specific programs, areas of emphasis, and personality traits of pastors varied greatly.

The second thing that struck me, after a little checking, was that an excellent Catholic Parish ten years ago might not be an excellent Catholic parish today. This confirmed our own experience. When enough people in a Parish are willing to care, it is as if the Holy Spirit decides to become more powerfully involved. I don't know how else to describe it. When enough people start taking their Parish for granted, thinking the status quo is good enough, wondering aloud why others aren't doing more, the Holy Spirit seems to slowly retreat. And what was so special no longer is. Parishes are like all the rest of God's creation. Nothing stays the same. Everything is in the process of becoming either more or less.

"But my Parish just isn't interesting." "There aren't enough caring people where I go to church." "Our pastor would never allow us to change anything." I hear these three common complaints from Roman Catholics who feel they are not part of active Parish communities. Clearly, some pastors are, for whatever reason, unwilling to consider any change, just as there are parishioners with the same view. Despite appearances, I believe both are exceptions.

Usually I just smile and nod when I hear one of these complaints. If I suspect the speaker might actually be interested in doing something about the problem, however, I suggest the following. Find something specific project that will benefit the Parish and can be completed in a finite timeframe. Ask the pastor if he minds your finding fellow parishioners to help you complete the project, along with raising whatever money may be needed. In almost every case, you will be surprised by how positive your pastor will be.

Once the project is completed, you will be surprised again. Your pastor will have other things he would like done, and if your association continues, there may even be things the two of you have dreamed of but never thought possible. You might even find your element.

The biggest problem pastors have with volunteer help is their dropout rate. Someone enthusiastically recommends a project or program, the pastor agrees, the volunteer begins but before long loses interest, leaving the pastor with one more thing to do, or a black eye for the Parish. Pastors are incredibly grateful for those who exhibit two traits: a willingness to follow through and humility when it comes to sharing credit.

When you are the one who takes responsibility for the successful completion of a project, you may be surprised again, this time by the reaction of your fellow workers. No matter how difficult or challenging a project is, everyone remembers a successful project as having been fun. And everyone who has experienced this kind of fun wants more. Small successes lead to larger ones, so long as those involved never forget that the goal is the Parish rather than personal gain.

Once this process is started, it soon becomes apparent there are plenty of caring people in every Parish. They just needed a little help to start uncovering their passion. In my introduction to Chapter III, "The Journey," I referenced my friend John. For several years John helped with the annual Parish Retreat at St. Peter's in the Florida Keys. He often remarked how special the people were there. Then John decided to become more active in his own Parish in Vermont. One night, in the midst of one of our never-ending debates, he mentioned he might not have time to do much more at St. Peter's. In becoming more involved in his own Parish, he had discovered there were also many very special people right there.

But even if I wanted to, how could I possibly change an entire Parish?

You don't have to change an entire Parish. You just have to change about five percent of those who attend Sunday Mass.

It has been my experience that approximately eighty percent of those who attend Sunday Mass consider this attendance their total commitment to Roman Catholicism. As a general rule, they attend most but not all Sundays. Their religious education stopped at some point during grade school, if they had any at all. A sense of obligation or family training is their primary motivation. This group is the "unchurched churched."

The remaining twenty percent have a higher attendance rate at Mass and do some form of volunteer work at or for the Parish, even though their religious education level is about the same. One quarter of these, or five percent of the total number of people attending Sunday Mass, do eighty to ninety-five percent of the work in a Parish. When this number is doubled to ten percent, it feels as if the Parish is on fire. And the prospects for this five percent show up every Sunday!

If the idea of even five percent seems daunting, remember you are only asked to make the effort, and keep making the effort, one person at a time, one project at a time, to make the Body of Christ a more visible reality. Once again, I think you will be surprised. For you have a pretty good partner in this endeavor. And the more you give....

Every so often someone asks me what I think the Roman Catholic Church will be like in the future. I answer by saying that, as always, the Pope, bishops and priests will play a role, for they are an important part of the Body of Christ. But they are only a part.

The primary determinant in what our Church will become is the larger Body of Christ. Will we, one by one, accept that we were baptized priest, prophet, and king, charged with being Christ to one another in a world desperate for his touch, so that we and they can experience more joy in our lives? Or will we continue to become less?

I live with hope. For we are the ones who will, in the end, answer the question, what is the future for our Church?

For You and Me

The word religion comes from the Latin *re ligare,* which means to reconnect.[268] For Christians, this was intended to acknowledge our need to reconnect with our God after the fall of Adam. In today's society, I think religion holds the potential to help us reconnect to the Divine, each other, and ourselves. This belief is grounded in my certainty that Jesus did not come to teach us Church orthodoxy. He came to teach us how to live life fully in preparation for living life perfectly in union with his Father. He came not to condemn but to save. By what he said and did, Jesus focused on how to live. For Roman Catholics, my belief is these teachings can help you and me reconnect with our God, each other, and ourselves. It is what I have experienced.

So the final part of my answer to the question "What will the future be?" is this: I hope this attempt at sharing my story will help other Catholic Christians, practicing and non-practicing, churched and unchurched, to reconnect. For we all have a largely unrecognized need for spiritual nourishment, without which I do not think it is possible to fully experience life, or for our Church to thrive.

I give thanks for those of you who have found this book helpful. For those of you who have not, I pray you will continue to search.

May God bless you all. And lead you to his joy.

---

268   *Deacon Digest,* July 2011 issue, p.21